PUT YOUR PANTS ON AND GET TO WORK

TEN PRINCIPLES FOR ZESTFUL LIVING

Kalman Magyar

Cover Design: Matt Dupuis - chickandowldesign.com

Contact: kalmanmagyar@yahoo.com

Table of Contents

ABOUT THE AUTHOR

Kalman Magyar has a remarkably eccentric skill set and atypical background. He is an international business lawyer and professor with over two decades of wide-ranging experience in courtrooms, boardrooms and classrooms throughout the United States and Canada. He is also a renowned Hungarian folk musician who has appeared in the world's most prominent performing venues and obscurest ethnic community halls.

Kalman guides you through his unusual personal history while decoding his ten principles for a zestful life. The adventure begins with his family's ordeals in war-ravaged Hungary. It continues as a first-generation immigrant in New Jersey. Valuable lessons are drawn from Kalman's unconventional development in the legal and musical fields. The odyssey is far from smooth, with failures, challenges and missteps along the way.

These experiences form the genesis of the principles that collectively provide a blueprint for living zestfully. All day, every day.

Married with three children, Kalman splits his time between Toronto, Ontario and Naples, Florida. Kalman also takes frequent trips to Budapest, Hungary, the land of his ancestors where his journey begins.

Read more at kalmanmagyar.com and mbollp.com.

FOREWORD

This book presents a collection of principles that know where they came from. Kalman's reverence for family history, Hungarian music and culture, and pragmatic principles for life and work combine into a zestful blend indeed!

When I first met Kalman and his wife, it was amidst hobnobbing with corporate supporters at an Olympic sport fundraiser in Toronto. They seemed a bit out of place – too down to earth in relation to the vibe of the room, I thought.

Their wide smiles broadcast a genuine warmth and created an air of welcomeness and space amidst the crowd (and as you'll read, Kalman works at this). That warmth is found throughout these pages, allowing for easy connection between his stories and your own life's journey.

Kalman has given us what he has to offer. He is not arrogant, he is not apologetic, he is true to his experience. He's a mentor at your side, gently encouraging you to keep promises to yourself and to see your own uniqueness for the niche opportunities it can present you in life.

He's the kindest kick in the butt you'll ever get – an incredible feat! And Kalman's humor grabs you in spots. His keen forward-moving energy leaves you with the sense that he's not always aware of how funny he is (the most satisfying kind of humor).

Some of us have to work harder than others to keep our lives zestful. It's easy to be dragged down by life's disappointments, but this book is a reminder to take heart and have courage. Kalman lets us in behind the "successful lawyer" stereotype to show us how to live our principles in all areas of our lives.

Kalman's ten principles are far ranging. From love to time-management, there's something in these pages that will resonate with where you've been, where you are, or where you're headed.

Jeremiah Brown

Silver Medallist in Rowing, Men's Eight - 2012 Summer Olympics (London)

Public Speaker & Author of *The 4 Year Olympian - From First Stroke to Olympic Medallist*

www.the4yearolympian.com

INTRODUCTION

I'm honored to have built a respectable international law practice. I'm privileged to have contributed in my own small way to the continued revival and reach of Hungarian folk music. Yet my greatest source of pride is that people I encounter, Jeremiah Brown included, can see that I'm authentically "zestful" – that is, happy, enthusiastic and energetic.

Knowing that I'm living zestfully in a way that's projected to others is more important than any accomplishment I'll ever achieve in law or music.

A zestful life is the great equalizer. It requires no special effort, skill, education, or money. All it takes is following these ten principles which universally apply to people of any age, background, location, political affiliation, religious belief, or social standing:

- Put Your Pants On and Get To Work

- Accept That Life Isn't Up and To the Right

- Find Your Calling

- Be Polite, Pleasant and Kind

- Honor Your Word

- Embrace Rejection

- Shoot Straight

- Keep Scanning

- Maintain Ready Position

- Craft Your Own Future

The principles did not appear out of thin air. As simple as they sound, they've been painstakingly established and honed over generations, resiliently surviving turbulent and jubilant times alike. In this book, I'll share with you their sources, how they guide me every day, and how they might be incorporated into your own life.

Understanding these principles and putting them into action will result in all the happiness, enthusiasm and energy you desire. No matter where you've been or where you're heading, that's a life worth living.

PRINCIPLE #1
PUT YOUR PANTS ON AND GET TO WORK

"Action is the foundational key to all success." - Pablo Picasso

Conor McCourt and Marguerite Ethier form one of the greatest power couples the legal profession has ever known. Both were partners at two preeminent Toronto law firms before retiring to Vancouver. When I worked as an in-house counsel, Conor was one of my company's outside lawyers and a world-class client relationship manager.

They have had a wonderfully active retirement traveling the world together. Marguerite, a masterful litigator, still does pro bono legal work for her favorite causes. Conor decided to pursue his long-time passion of cooking. He went to chef school in Vancouver and now volunteers his time cooking at community soup kitchens.

These are outstanding people. Super lawyers and super humans. Role models.

During his training, Conor was the oldest student. One of his 20-some-thing-year-old classmates asked him one day, "What was your greatest secret to success as a lawyer"? That's a great question. How did he rise to the top of the legal food chain?

Conor's unflinching answer to the inquiring culinary mind: "Every morning, I just got up and went to work."

The singular ingredient to success for one of Canada's most accomplished big-firm partners? Just get up and get to work. And keep getting to work daily.

Notice what Conor does not refer to. No discussion of specialized expert knowledge, even though Conor has gobs of it. No reference to pulling all-nighters, being lucky, navigating complex partner dynamics, or getting invoices out on time. All of these are important for success in the legal profession, but Conor's key advice is to just get out of bed, show up and get to work.

"Success" will follow.

I prefer to re-state Conor's advice a little differently – put your pants on and get to work. These are the two simple physical acts that will put you on the path to a zestful life:

• putting pants on, or whatever you might wear to start your day

• getting to work, no matter what or where your work may be

"Work" is a general term that could refer to your day-job or educational studies. But it can also mean exercising, reading, writing, responding to the day's first email, or even just making your bed. Only you know what "work" means in your own individual context each day. Some retiree friends in Florida understand this concept completely, treating their tennis, golf, card playing, and social gatherings as their work.

This principle is not about waking up early. And it's not about wearing fancy pants or being involved in world-changing work. It's about taking action by simply showing up. Every day.

Are you surprised at how simple Conor's advice sounds? Don't be. Never underestimate other people's capability to be lazy and irresponsible. For those of you who put your pants on and get to work daily, it might very well be the only competitive edge or survival skill you'll ever need. Expect most people not to bother to do even that much.

This is such a basic and crucial daily practice that it's the title of this book. Each principle that follows flows from this first step.

LOOK TO YOUR FAMILY HISTORY FOR INSPIRATION

Most family histories are likely full of examples of people who consistently got dressed and went to work. Digging into your ancestors' experiences might serve as inspiration as you look to apply the principles in this book.

My family's history is rooted in Hungary. The country's foundation goes back to the year 896. After a series of foreign occupations and shifting borders, today it is roughly equivalent to Portugal's size and population, with about 10 million inhabitants, but in the center of Europe, five countries to the east of Portugal. Hungary has punched above its weight on the global stage, offering an unusually large number of inventors, scientists, artists, and athletes. Famous Hungarians you might have heard of are Ernő Rubik (inventor of the Rubik's Cube), Ferenc Puskás (at one time the world's greatest soccer player),

Andy Grove (Silicon Valley pioneer), Albert Szent-Györgyi (discoverer of vitamin C), and composers Franz Liszt and Béla Bartók.

My great-grandfather, Zygmund Piatek, was from the city of Rzeszów, Poland. While Zygmund wasn't Hungarian, Rzeszów was once part of the Galicia province in the Austro-Hungarian Empire. The Empire was formed in 1867, the same year as Canada, as a dual monarchy between Austria and the "Kingdom of Hungary" which stretched from Galicia to the north all the way down to the Dalmatian coast of Croatia. The Empire was dismantled after losing in World War I, reducing the area of Hungary to its current size.

Zygmund was an officer in the Austro-Hungarian Army during the War. He was stationed in Magyaróvár, a Hungarian town close to the Austrian border now known as Mosonmagyaróvár. That's where Zygmund met his wife, an elementary school teacher named Melánia Redle. They became the parents of my grandmother, Olga Piatek. She was born in Magyaróvár in April 1918, the year World War I ended and the Spanish flu pandemic began.

1918 must have been quite a year in Europe. Just wrapping up a world war? Congrats. Now here's a pandemic to keep you busy for the next few years.

Zygmund took his family to Rzeszów after World War I ended. A few years later, though, Melánia and Zygmund divorced. She returned to Magyaróvár with her children. Their daughter Olga eventually moved to Hungary's capital, Budapest. Nearly a third of Hungary's population lives in the Budapest metropolitan area. It's a gorgeous city, with the oldest subway system in continental Europe and the world's third largest and perhaps most alluring parliament building resting on the banks of the Danube (Duna), Europe's second longest river. The Danube separates Buda on its west and Pest on its east sides, joined together by a dazzling set of elegant bridges.

Olga met and married my grandfather and became a secretary for some well-known professors at the University of Technology (Műszaki Egyetem), located on the Buda side of the Liberty Bridge (Szabadság Híd). She emigrated to the U.S. with her daughter, my mom, in 1963. Unfortunately I never met Olga. She died of breast cancer at the age of 54, a year before I was born.

DON'T DWELL ON YOUR MISFORTUNES

There are days when life kicks us in the butt and we'd rather not put our pants on, much less get to work. Often this is the result of some kind of misfortune.

Misfortune is different than a failure. When you fail at something, it's usually never a wasted effort. You're able to learn from each failure, which in turn makes you better at whatever you are trying to achieve.

On the other hand, misfortune cruelly comes out of nowhere. Life takes a big dump on you and you had nothing to do with it. During such difficult dark days, I think about the plight of my grandmother Sarolta, whose whole life started with a significant misfortune.

Sarolta's dad, my great-grandfather Dusán Jovanovits, was an ethnic Serb born in Perlez, Vojvodina (Vajdaság), which used to be a part of the Austro-Hungarian Empire. He grew up in nearby Zrenjanin, which back in his day was known as Bečkerek (Nagybecskerek in Hungarian).

The son of a Serbian Orthodox priest, Dusán spoke Serbian and Hungarian fluently. He worked as a stationmaster for the Austro-Hungarian railway system. This work took him to the Great Plain (Alföld) in southern Hungary near Kiskunhalas, Hungary, a city which serves as an important junction on the Budapest-Belgrade railway line. That's where he met Julianna Valkai, my great-grandmother. Her family was rooted in that area for many generations, mostly engaged in typical agricultural activities.

Dusán and Julianna got married. Julianna became pregnant. A healthy man in his early 30's, Dusán was drafted into the Austro-Hungarian army. While Julianna was pregnant, he was sent to army training.

Dusán was captured by Russian troops at the start of World War I, though we don't have details of where or how. He was sent to a prisoner of war (POW) camp in Siberia, where he died probably in 1915, like most of the half-million Austrian-Hungarian POWs captured by the Russians. Whether he was executed, froze to death or died from disease, we'll never know.

According to history books, at least 20 million people died during World War I. 20 million! Dusán's abrupt death was certainly not unique at that time. Still, I shudder to think about poor Julianna, with a baby at home, waiting for news about Dusán – any news whatsoever. But it never came. Her husband just vanished off the face of the earth.

Julianna never remarried, and her daughter Sarolta never met her father. This is, by any measure, exactly the type of hardship that could greatly sidetrack a young person's life. Rather than dwell on this lamentable misfortune, Sarolta would grow up to be tougher than her peers. She became determined to carve out her own way despite the odds. I'll describe later how that happened.

WORKING ON THE SIZE OF PANTS

It's time to flip this principle around. Rather than talk about putting on pants and getting to work, I'll describe how I got to work on reducing the size of my pants. Perhaps my experience will be of some use to you.

Healthy eating has been an especially daunting challenge in my life. I spent decades in the middle of the "obese" body mass index (BMI) range. Intellectually I'm fully read up about diet and exercise, but you don't learn to ride a bike by reading about it. Instead, like most everyone, I like fried foods, chips, chocolate, and alcohol. I don't like to work out. Most of the day I sit at a desk. I have an active social life which includes going out for dinners. Though my vitals have generally been good, my weight suffered. Not even my wife could compel me to change my ways, even though she's an accomplished and popular fitness trainer.

Then, at the age of 45, I started losing weight effectively. Once experiencing some momentum, I kept with the plan, lost more than 50 pounds over a year, and achieved a "normal" BMI. I have even managed to keep the extra weight off, two years later.

Never take nutrition advice from a lawyer, much less a musician, so this is not meant to be advice. However, I am happy to share the simplicity of how I got to work on reducing my pant size:

STEP 1: Immediately after my first daily visit to the bathroom, I weighed myself.

STEP 2: Wrote down my weight for that day.

STEP 3: Ate and drank normally for breakfast and lunch.

STEP 4: Had a light snack (fruit, veggie, nuts) at around 4:00 pm.

STEP 5: Only drank water after 4:00 pm, didn't eat or drink anything else.

STEP 6: Avoided the kitchen, went to sleep, woke up the next day skinnier.

I like this plan because the only special know-how required is deciphering when it is 4:00 pm. We all know how to do that and it doesn't require any extra work. Obviously, I lost more weight faster by avoiding high carbs, alcohol and dessert. But an incremental 0.2 lb. daily weight loss is still a loss and added up over time.

UNDERSTAND YOUR WORK

We can't go to work just for the sake of working. Some basic competence in our chosen line of business needs to be established. As TED Talks celebrity speaker Simon Sinek cautions in *Start With Why: How Great Leaders Inspire Everyone to Take Action*: "Start with why, but know how."

Speaking of TED, my friend Ted Mangnall knows his trade intimately. He started working at Canadian Tire as a teenager and climbed his way through the ranks over many years. For those that don't know, the retail giant Canadian Tire is one of the country's most treasured super-authentic and super-Canadian institutions, like Tim Hortons, Roots and Toronto potholes.

Ted is now a Canadian Tire dealer, owning and operating one of the brand's largest stores in Canada. During one of our many talks about the business world, Ted truncated everything he knows about running a retail operation into three basic steps:

- stock shelves

- smile at customers when they pay

- re-stock shelves

I love the clarity of boiling down complex businesses in such simple points. Ted's summary says it all in terms of operating a big-box retail outfit, from inventory control (sales) to customer satisfaction (service). Keeping business models simple allows operators to stay on track. By simplifying we're better able to cope with the ebb-and-flow and the daily drama that comes with business life, whether you're a proprietor or employee.

Unfortunately, two of my great-grandparents learned their lessons in business the hard way. It's not enough to put on pants and get to work. We also need to have at least some level of proficiency in our work.

My father's ascendants were generally such peasants that, as the Hungarian saying goes, they even ate their ice cream using a pocketknife. Kálmán Magyar II, my dad's grandfather, owned a small mill in Zsana. His wife, my great-grandmother Terézia Tóth, was a wonderful cook with magical culinary skills Conor McCourt would envy. After Kálmán's II mill was destroyed in a fire, the family moved back to Kiskunhalas. They decided to leap into business and open a small pub. It sounded like a cool undertaking at the time.

The pub was an epic failure and the reason was simple. No one explained to them the importance of getting customers to pay their tabs. The pub's finances unraveled thanks to the regulars who took advantage of my great-grandparents' naïve generosity and lack of service business acumen. My great-grandparents tried to run their pub like social hosts rather than a profitable business. They didn't have the resources of TED Talks or Ted Mangnall to set them straight. These folks knew how to put on their pants. They sometimes just didn't know exactly how to execute their work.

Putting on pants and getting to work requires perseverance and tenacity. No one knew this more than my grandmother Sarolta Jovanovits who once had her future predicted by a Roma fortune teller. The fortune teller boldly shared her vision that my grandmother, who was born in Kiskunhalas in June 1913, would one day end up working in New York. From the Great Hungarian Plain to New York? This was a far stretch for a poor village hairdresser raised by a single mother. But this premonition, however far-fetched, came true. It wasn't because of luck. It was tenacity.

Sarolta's journey started when she married Kálmán III, my grandfather. Their first kids were twin girls who were so distinctly beautiful that their images were painted on the frescoes on the ceiling of the Kiskunhalas Catholic Church – posing as angels, no less. When my father, born six years after the twins, was quite young, the family moved to larger nearby Szeged where Sarolta had found work as a hairdresser with the Szeged National Theater (Szegedi Nemzeti Színház). Her next stop was the wig department of the renowned Madách Theater in Budapest, Hungary's answer to Broadway.

Sarolta was certainly good at her job as a hairdresser and wig maker, though there was more to her somewhat meteoric rise from small village to Hungary's Broadway than talent alone. At a time when males dominated the workplace and drove family decision-making, she was an absolute steamroller.

Once in Budapest, Sarolta secured an apartment for the family in the middle of Pest, a block from the famous Vörösmarty Square. She managed to get the twin girls accepted into the prestigious Hungarian National Ballet School in Budapest. Though my dad much preferred to play soccer and get into trouble, Sarolta used her connections and had him admitted into the Ballet School as well, at the tender age of nine. There was no saying "no" to Sarolta.

Then came the Revolution of October 1956 in which Hungary attempted to rid itself of the Soviet-controlled post-World War II communist government. Sarolta and her family had a front-row view of the tanks rolling in and out of Budapest from their downtown apartment. The Revolution ultimately failed and their beloved Hungary was in tatters. Sarolta and her twin daughters left the country a few days after the Revolution concluded and ended up in the U.S. They were just three of the approximately 200,000 who fled the country in the Revolution's immediate aftermath. My grandfather and my dad stayed in Budapest to care for my great-grandmother Terézia who was sick and couldn't travel. The Kálmáns only put in their travel paperwork for the U.S. after she died several years later.

My grandmother had significant cardiac problems, suffering multiple health issues as she was aging. Her last hemorrhage was catastrophic. She died in 1995 in Rockville, Maryland. Sarolta was extraordinarily strong, confident and hilarious. Her life underscores that sheer resolve can take you places you couldn't imagine.

Sarolta was one of my early champions. She made me feel like I could do anything and be anything I wanted to be. I'll never forget one piece of sage advice she gave me before she died, which was that she wanted me to get a job where I would carry a briefcase to work rather than a set of tools. That, for her, would be "success."

She died a few weeks after I started attending law school, hopefully knowing that I was well on the way to making good on her advice.

TOMORROW IS WAITING

My university buddy, Franco, signed up for an introductory Italian class during college. Unfortunately for him, the class ended up being scheduled for 8:30 am and he was a night-owl. He could never wake up on time. Franco failed the class.

Yet Franco was the son of Italian immigrants and already spoke Italian fluently. Had he just shown up for class, he would have passed with flying colors without burning a calorie. He thought he'd get some easy credits but didn't consider the impact of the class's start time on his attendance.

Franco didn't put on his pants and get to work.

Have you ever pulled a Franco and blown off the day? I sure have. And I'm sure the retired illustrious lawyer and volunteer chef Conor McCourt has as well. But rest easy, tomorrow is a new day. A fresh set of pants are waiting for you.

Pablo Picasso's quote at the beginning of this chapter reminds us that without action we can't have success. The meaning of "success" might surprise you, though. The next principle explains why.

PRINCIPLE #2
ACCEPT THAT LIFE ISN'T UP AND TO THE RIGHT

"Success is a journey, not a destination; the doing is often more important than the outcome." - Arthur Ashe

When viewing the progress of our lives in a graph, it's not going to be up and to the right. It'll be a down-up-down-up-plateau-up-down type of freakish roller coaster looking thing. This is the case no matter what criteria we might look at, such as income, accolades, debt, trophies, quality of relationships, and health.

I've had two bad financial experiences over the last several years. First, a contractor working on our Toronto home ended up being a complete swindler. Everything we paid him for had to be redone. Though we sued him and have a civil judgment against him, we'll never be able to collect on it. You can't draw blood from a stone. We lost a wad of money on that con-man and we won't get it back.

Just as my wife and I were starting to dig out from that hole, I was retained as a lawyer in a litigation that ended up going sideways. I can't disclose details of most of my legal work in this book because of privilege and confidentiality issues, but everything that could go wrong in a case did. It was a perfect storm of heated litigants, diabolical lawyers, unfavorable court decisions, and uncooperative insurance companies. I got stuck in the middle of this storm and had to pay major dollars as part of a global resolution to help bring the mess to a necessary close. This settlement set us back quite substantially again.

My wife and I have tried our best to be cheerful despite these financial challenges. In fact, only a very few of our friends and family would have any reason to know either of these events happened or how they affected us.

Don't focus on a particular outcome or specific place at any fixed point in time on life's graph. If you do, you will struggle to get through the lows and lose perspective at the top. One of my favorite books, Dr. Richard Carlson's *Don't Sweat the Small Stuff*, is dedicated to the subject of dealing with these ups and downs. It's the perfect title and one of the secrets of a zestful life.

Your challenges will be easier to digest and manage if you accept that life isn't up and to the right. We can't measure "success" that way. Instead, our "success" comes from doing what we know we're supposed to be doing. And that means sticking to the principles described in this book, because they're the sources of a happy and energetic life. Not your latest results, stumbling blocks or awards.

OVERCOME DOWN AND TO THE LEFT WITH DIGNITY

The saga of the fourth and final set of my great-grandparents is probably the closest there is in my family to a "riches-to-rags" story. They experienced life on the way up the roller coaster, at the top of the roller coaster, and on the way down too.

And that's the moment – when life seems patently unfair – to remember to keep riding that roller coaster with dignity.

My great-grandfather, Károly Mikecz, came from aristocratic stock in the city of Nyíregyháza in northeast Hungary. A law graduate turned banker, Károly became a director of the Hungarian National Central Savings Bank (MOKTÁR). He met his wife, Judit Vámossy, in the fanciful social circles of Budapest. They were among the upper echelon of old-money blue-bloods waltzing away in the capital city before the music stopped and it all came tumbling down.

Judit's brother, Tibor Vámossy, was a 19 year-old engineering student in 1921 when he was shot to death by an Austrian patrolman during the Western Hungarian Uprising which resulted in Hungary reclaiming a small portion of land it had originally lost after World War I. Tibor was the only remaining male bearing the Vámossy name. Károly and Judit's eldest son took on the last name, becoming János Vámossy-Mikecz. János, my grandfather, lived the longest of all my grandparents.

Though my grandfather took over the Vámossy name, he liked telling a story about how prevalent the famed Mikecz name was in Nyíregyháza. When Franz Joseph I, the Emperor of Austria-Hungary, once visited Nyíregyháza, he was greeted by a long line of men who introduced themselves as "Mikecz" this and "Mikecz" that. Towards the end of the greeting line a young boy also introduced himself as "Mikecz," after which Franz Joseph I exclaimed, "oh my, such a young child and already a Mikecz." The King thought the ubiquitous "Mikecz" was a title rather than a family name!

Hungary was on the losing side of World War II, as it was in World War I. The loss ushered in the Soviet presence and influence that would last for over four decades. By the end of World War II, the ruling communists were busy taking punitive measures against the upper class. Though Judit and Károly were divorced by the end of the war, their wealth was "redistributed" and their families were "relocated." These are code words for having assets seized and being banished to the rural countryside. This was the new government's design to try to even further strip them of their stature. This would be the fate of many after the war.

Károly was sent to work at a chicken farm. Judit had married another upper-class gentleman, Dénes Stromszky de Nemeskolta, son of the former managing director of Siemens' operation in Hungary. They were sent to a farm too. It was a rather magnificent fall from grace.

People in their situation had every reason to wallow in their humiliation and new-found poverty. But they bit their lips and persevered. Their reward came when the two families were eventually allowed back to Budapest, though their assets were never fully regained. My great-grandparents got along well and spent much of their remaining days in Leányfalu, an idyllic town north of Budapest on the banks of the Danube which became the large extended family's consistent central hub.

Life is going to throw all kinds of curveballs at us. My Mikecz relatives had a good dose of these, from fraternizing with the Emperor to being forced to work as chicken farmers. They maintained their dignity and held their heads up high. Things ended up just fine for them and their families despite their substantial setbacks. It's because they never stopped living gracefully, no matter what fate had in store for them.

CONSIDER CARVING OUT YOUR OWN NICHE

Sometimes it feels like fate is conspiring against us. No matter how hard we try, obstacles for our advancement are everywhere. Rather than walk the usual path or adhere to conventional wisdom, it might be a good time to consider carving out a niche.

My resolute grandmother knew this concept well and put it into practice within weeks of emigrating to the U.S. In doing so, she changed the course of my family's history.

After leaving Hungary, Sarolta arrived in New York with one of her daughters, Magda. (Magda's twin sister, Mária, went to Sweden with her boyfriend.) Following their release from the refugee processing camp at which they were required to sojourn after their arrival, they stayed in Philadelphia with a distant relative. My grandmother didn't speak English and she couldn't find suitable work. The relative was of no help either.

That's when Sarolta hatched a plan to carve out her own niche. She took a train ride to New York and found the Metropolitan Opera House. She located the backstage entrance and said to the security guard "Hungarian, opera."

The mystified security guard fetched the only Hungarian person he knew at the Met – Gábor Carelli, a well-known Hungarian tenor who was in a rehearsal on stage. My grandmother explained to Gábor that she was an experienced wig maker who just arrived from Hungary. Gábor immediately shuffled her over to the wig department and helped translate the discussion with the department's head. There was no one in-house at the Met who could make wigs. The "wig" department personnel were prepping and putting wigs and beards on singers, but they were being imported from West Germany and Italy. Because these creations were all handmade, there were substantial delays in having them made and shipped. It was a major logistical issue.

To test her skills, the head of the wig department asked my grandmother to make a moustache. My grandmother had her tools with her and completed it in 15 minutes. The lady couldn't believe her eyes.

My grandmother was immediately offered a full-time wig making job at the Met, right on the spot. The Met even paid for her temporary hotel stay until she found an apartment in the city.

Virtually all of the crew at the Met belonged to unions. Sarolta had enough of the unionized atmosphere in communist Hungary and refused to join the Union of Make-Up Artists & Hair Stylists. However, she had such a specialized skill no one else had, she was allowed to continue to work at the Met for decades without union membership. Unfortunately, this meant that when she retired, she would not receive the sweet union pension.

Sarolta's daughter, Magda, joined her later at the Met. Properly part of the union, Magda eventually became the head of the wig department. Magda's daughter, Juliet, also worked in the wig department until retiring in 2019. Even my dad worked at the Met, as an usher, during university.

My grandmother's ability to generate instant demand for her unique skills in a foreign country landed her a foot in the Met's door. This provided her with financial security and brought about 62 years of a connection between my family and the world's greatest opera company.

And in the process, Sarolta had made good on a Roma fortune teller's implausible prediction that she'd end up working in New York City.

SMILE

Smiling through peaks and valleys is something we can utilize to endure life's wild journey. Enter Kálmán III, my grandfather.

Kálmán III was born in the microscopic village of Zsana, Hungary in November 1907 and grew up in Kiskunhalas. When he and Sarolta relocated to Szeged, Kálmán III became the owner of a small drugstore. He did better in business than his parents. The ladies around town loved visiting and chatting with him about his cosmetic creations. He had a cheery disposition and a positive aura. His movie-star good looks certainly helped too.

Then, like many others, the drugstore was suddenly "nationalized" – or, more accurately, expropriated without compensation – by the communists in the early 1950's. He had no choice but to start working in a factory for the rest of his time in Hungary.

Kálmán III emigrated to the U.S. with my dad in 1962, but never learned English other than the basic hello, goodbye, thank you, and "no speak English." He did have some odd-jobs working in restaurants, cleaning movie theaters and designing plastics at a manufacturing plant. Of course, they were all Hungarian-owned businesses with no language requirements.

Nevertheless, just like back in Szeged, my grandfather was well-liked by those he interacted with because he was always smiling. When he went to the supermarket in New Jersey, the check-out ladies would often start talking to him, going on-and-on about something or other, while he just stood there silently and smiled, not understanding a word. One time he was joined at the store by my dad and the ladies commented, "Your father is such a nice guy."

Sometimes it only takes a smile. Think about it – without a word, my grandfather made connections with strangers just by smiling and not interrupting them. It made him a "nice guy." Smiling kept him centered and content in a foreign land. And it was certainly part of his popularity with his female customers in Szeged, where he fully spoke the language.

My grandfather was very crafty with his hands and I vividly recall him toiling away in his basement workshop, humming and singing to himself. He was a wiz with plastics and would spend weeks constructing plastic figurines, even creating a full chess set.

He also loved music. He made several zithers and even deconstructed a piano to design a homemade cimbalom (hammered dulcimer), an extraordinary feat. Kálmán III was a self-taught violinist and helped me develop a fascination for playing music when I was young. He attended my first music concerts and accompanied my sister and me when we started playing together.

My grandfather was the best cook in the family. His specialty was Hungarian peasant food, which emphasizes lots of grease and fat. He reveled in the joys of pork rinds, pig's ears and fried dough. While he was always a physically active and seemingly fit man, his choice of diet was ultimately detrimental to his heart.

In the winter of 1983, Kálmán III suffered a massive heart attack while shoveling snow. He died a few days later in the hospital. When thinking of him, I can't help but smile.

CREATE ECHOES OF KINDNESS

If you're on an upswing in life, remember that it won't last forever. This is an opportune time to create echoes of kindness to help others who might not be at the top of life's roller coaster.

Mother Teresa reminds us: "Kind words can be short and easy to speak, but their echoes are truly endless." When we open our mouths, we should try our best to say kind things, particularly when things are going well. Create positive echoes, especially from the top of the roller coaster.

I once had the opportunity to deliver a lecture on legal ethics for a business class at Parsons School's Fashion Design Department in New York, where an old friend was a professor. At the time, Tim Gunn was the Department's Chair. My friend arranged for a brief meeting with Mr. Gunn, who was already a reality TV celebrity through his popular show, Project Runway. I was a nervous wreck meeting this profoundly elegant titan of his industry. As we entered his office, Mr. Gunn was as chic and refined as I expected. The smell of expensive cologne was in the air. He didn't say much. In the three minutes or so we spent together, he simply thanked me for speaking with the students and said it meant a lot for the school to have me there. I'm sure he said the same thing to all guest lecturers. But the words had such a jolt of authenticity and kindness that they had a lasting impact on me.

I credit Mr. Gunn's encouragement for increasing my interest in teaching. After meeting him, I served as an adjunct civil litigation professor at Fairleigh Dickinson University in New Jersey. I continued teaching business law courses at Seneca College in Toronto. Now I'm an adjunct professor at Keiser University's Naples, Florida campus and serve as a mentor and moot court judge at the University of Toronto's Faculty of Law.

Years later, I saw Mr. Gunn at Toronto's Pearson airport. He was barely recognizable in his shorts and sandals. This is the author of *A Guide to Quality, Taste & Style*, a book I actually own! It's refreshing to see that even he's not always dressed to the nines.

Teaching is a natural extension of my fondness for performing within an academic setting. There's no better way to strengthen knowledge in a subject matter than by teaching it to others. We learn more by teaching than by being a student. Mr. Gunn's kind words, however ephemeral and even generic, have created endless echoes which have benefitted me as a professor and, in turn, my pupils. What lasting power the tiniest of kind words have, especially when uttered from the top of life's roller coaster.

MAKE BIG CHANGES IF THE LOWS PERSIST

Sometimes a drastic change is needed to start climbing upwards again. This strategy was implemented by my grandfather, János (John) Vámossy-Mikecz, who was born in April 1916 in the midst of World War I. He had the good fortune of having a stellar education and enjoyed a career as a foreign business correspondent in Budapest and a junior diplomat in France.

Once the communists came to power after World War II, his rising career came to a crashing halt, as he was the descendant of aristocratic families whose assets and status had been ripped away after the war. János was "demoted" to the role of a night watchman at a state-run farm. Forced labor on farms was becoming an unfortunate theme in the Vámossy-Mikecz experience.

The writing of an unpromising future in Hungary was on the wall. János and his family were the victims of sudden regime change and were being dragged into lowliness. He was young and knew he needed to make a considerable change in order to climb upwards again.

János and his teenaged son quietly slipped out of the country on November 26, 1956, a few days after the end of the Revolution. They hitched a ride on the back of a truck to the Austrian border and negotiated dangerous minefields and fences on their way to freedom. After spending a few weeks in an Austrian "displaced persons" camp, they sailed by U.S. Army ship to New York in January 1957.

My grandfather spoke five languages, including English. He declined to speak Russian, though he knew how. And he refused to drink vodka. This was a silent protest against anything having to do with the Soviets who drove him out of his homeland.

His education and language knowledge enabled János to transition pretty smoothly in his new country. He ended up working as a bookkeeper in New York, most notably at the Bank of America. Spending time in New York's vibrant Hungarian social circles reminded him of the good old days in Budapest.

My grandmother, Olga, and János were both children of divorced parents. Perhaps it didn't come as a surprise that János and Olga divorced when my mother was a toddler. Each remarried briefly but those marriages ended in divorce, too.

They re-wed each other after the family's 1963 reunification in New York, but they soon separated for a second time. Their attempt to give it another shot was definitely laudable.

János was my only grandparent to see me graduate from law school and get married. He was an expert in nature and world politics. His retirement consisted of traveling, birdwatching and engrossing himself in what seemed like hundreds of books about twentieth century history.

But the highlight of his retirement was a solo three-month minivan road trip throughout the U.S. It was his way of showing gratitude to the country that gave him a much-needed second chance in life. János died in 2004 after battling prostate cancer for years, a few months after he held my first child after her birth.

THE MEANING OF "SUCCESS"

Though it doesn't hurt, money alone doesn't make you happy. I have interacted with service workers in banquet hall kitchens as a musician and with eight-figure earning tycoons as a lawyer. In the process, I've met miserable people who are "rich" and happy people who are "poor." Meeting others, you never know what their salaries are or how much debt they're in. People don't disclose their account balances or mortgage statements, but you can immediately tell if they are zestful, and it has nothing to do with what's in those documents.

People who seem genuinely happy and kind seem skilled at navigating life's peaks and valleys. They internalize this message from the Old Testament: "You are dust and to dust you shall return." As Arthur Ashe's quote at the beginning of this chapter reminds us, our "success" lies in the journey and not the destination.

Forget "up and to the right," it's not based in reality. Get comfortable with that concept and you will make space for a consistently zestful life. That's the meaning of "success."

PRINCIPLE #3
FIND YOUR CALLING

"The two most important days in your life are the day you are born and the day you find out why." - Mark Twain

Everyone needs a calling. A calling is something usually other than your full-time job that keeps your inner fire lit, consumes your free time, and is your way to give back to the world. It's the reason you exist.

I've witnessed people without a calling often lack an inner fire, ambition or aspiration.

It's important to distinguish your calling from your passion. I am passionate about watching soccer and drinking whiskey. Preferably at the same time. Neither of those is a calling. A calling is something most people would agree gives purpose to you while creating value for others.

If you don't have a calling, find one. It's so important that it's one of the key principles for zestful living.

YOUR CALLING CAN CHANGE THE WORLD

My father, Kálmán Magyar IV, was born in Kiskunhalas on January 24, 1945, in the midst of the heaviest bombing of World War II. Perhaps all of the pandemonium at the time of his birth was the cause of my dad's allergy to silence and lifelong dedication to performing.

After moving to Budapest as a young boy, he trained with the Hungarian National Ballet School. He was athletic with a keen sense of rhythm. However, he was cut as part of the School's vetting process soon after his mother and older twin sisters left Hungary in 1956. He then embarked on years of rebellious mischief, as his father worked in a factory trying to make ends meet.

So passed his teenage years during which my dad, the quintessential class clown, perfected the art of entertaining. He left his friends and classmates in stitches and his teachers and grandmothers who looked after him in bewilderment. Today he probably would have been diagnosed as hyperactive and medicated, but back then he was just made to sit in a corner and whipped with a ruler or, in Hungarian style, with a wooden spoon.

My dad's days of tomfoolery ended in 1962, after he and his father received permission to leave Hungary and fly to New York to join the rest of the family. My dad was 17 years old when he and his father landed at JFK Airport. Neither spoke English when my dad appeared at the principal's office at George Washington High School on his first day of class. On the P.A. system, the principal asked for anyone who spoke Hungarian to report to the office to help translate the discussion. Another Hungarian-speaking student quickly appeared in the office.

After hearing about my dad's Ballet Academy experience, the translating student immediately invited him to join the newly-established "Hungária" Folkdance Ensemble, which was practicing weekly in New York. The group was teeming with young, energetic post-1956 Revolution immigrants. They immediately took in my father, with his superior dance talent and big-stage performing experience. His short-lived ballet career as a youngster in Budapest came in handy.

My father immersed himself into Hungarian folkdance and eventually became the group's director. He went on to teach folkdance throughout the U.S. Through the vessel of his non-profit American Hungarian Folklore Centrum, he has showcased our culture and helped put Hungarian folklore on the map in North America, even to this day.

Parallel to these activities, my father managed to get through high school while taking crash-courses in English. He studied chemistry in university and worked his way up the corporate ladder as a regulatory affairs specialist in the pharmaceutical and medical devices industries. Later he transitioned into packaging equipment and supplies and founded the company AMCO in Budapest. It is now one of Hungary's top packaging distributors.

But my dad's calling will forever remain the performing arts. He has organized hundreds of tours, performances and exhibitions of Hungarian artists, musicians and dancers over five decades all over the U.S. and Canada. I can safely say that hundreds of thousands of people have received the benefit of his work. So will future generations. My father's dedication to his calling has positively changed the world.

MONETIZE YOUR CALLING, UNLESS YOU SHOULDN'T

Businesses often have callings. In his introduction to *Onward*, Starbucks' former CEO Howard Schultz writes: "As a business leader, my quest has never been just about winning or making money; it has also been about building a great, enduring company, which has always meant trying to strike a balance between profit and social conscience." It's wonderful when a corporation has such an exalted calling. And it also explains why we might be paying so much for a tall blonde coffee at Starbucks.

Sometimes your calling in life might be your full-time job. If that happens, you might not even call it a "job" at all. It would be great if this was always the case, but it doesn't usually happen. Tennis legend Andre Agassi famously revealed in his autobiography, *Open*, that he hated playing tennis (his job) until he realized how it could be leveraged to support the creation of a charter school for children in need (his calling).

I used to belong to a tennis club in Toronto where a highly entertaining character from the former Yugoslavia was the lead court attendant. He used to mock the parents who thought their children would become the next Andre Agassi or Serena Williams. He'd tease them by saying he had a better chance of winning the lottery than their kids becoming tennis stars.

But wouldn't you know it – and this is 100% true – the tennis court attendant ended up winning the Lotto 6/49 jackpot of $8 Million in 2017.

Having passion for something is fantastic, but unless you have that kind of lottery-winning luck, at least some talent is generally required to monetize it.

In 1983, the Suburbanite, a small New Jersey newspaper, ran a "From the mouths of babes" feature, asking fourth graders the question, "What would you like to be doing 25 years from now?" My response was one of the ones printed:

"Magyar shoots and a GOAL!" That's my future. I would like to be a soccer player. I would be a sweeper as Beckenbauer is today. I would be playing with the Cosmos.

When I have retired, I would have a lot of money. I would buy a big house, with six bedrooms, three bathrooms, and four TV's. I would have a Hungarian maid.

I would start playing violin in private (as I do now). During this time, I would move to somewhere in Europe and continue to play the violin.

My early soccer dreams never became a reality. My career came to a crashing halt as a back-up defender on my high school's freshman soccer team when scoring a brilliant goal off of a corner kick during a pre-season game, beating my own keeper. This drew the ire of my coach who preferred to see me on the bench after that.

Around the same time, I had switched from studying violin to viola, a slightly larger version of the violin but an entirely different instrument nonetheless. My teacher was demanding that I choose between soccer and viola. My viola practice time was suffering. I quit the soccer team, making room for a calling in which I actually have talent.

I started to consider the possibility of becoming a full-time, professional classical musician. Perhaps I could have played viola in the orchestra of the Metropolitan Opera, where I'd spent many mesmerizing nights while growing up, thanks to free last-minute standing room tickets through my aunt's connections. Or maybe in a symphony orchestra somewhere in Europe. I had the talent, time and financial support from my parents to make it happen. But I was missing the relationship with practicing that was necessary to be a full-time professional musician. That relationship is the determining factor for becoming an elite performer.

I'll never forget the ninth-grade violinist in my orchestra at music school who received detention for cutting classes from his regular (non-music) school. He cut classes because he stayed home and practiced while his parents were at work. That is dedication. I could never develop that kind of connection with practicing.

As I was growing up, my parents' home was a revolving door of musicians, dancers and other artists from Hungary. Our home served as their central hub while touring in the U.S. on trips organized by my parents. Most of them specialized in the folk genre and there were many sleepless nights with legendary parties which brought together these folk luminaries and the members of our local immigrant community. Waking up finding fully-grown adults snoring in sleeping bags on our living room floor was a frequent occurrence.

One of my musical mentors and family friends, Attila Falvay, is a much more subdued fellow. Though his father was folk dancer, Attila is a highly accomplished and well-known Hungarian classical violinist. When I was a young teenager, he stayed at our house while touring with the world-famous Kodály Quartet. His daily practicing routine was something to behold: About 90 minutes of scales; roughly two hours of etudes and exercises; and who knows how many hours of working on pieces. And it was careful, self-critically painstaking practicing. Attila agonized over every note, every string-crossing, every breath, every interpretation. I'm sure he loved every minute. Listening to him, I knew the regimen wasn't for me.

Developing a relationship with practicing is important for not just classical musicians, but those in other genres too. I saw the famous jazz violinist Stéphane Grappelli play at New York's Blue Note a few years before he died. Even at an advanced age, he had perfect intonation which can only come from the most meticulous form of highly disciplined practicing. Louis Armstrong may have smoked reams of weed, but he is also famously quoted as saying: "If I don't practice for a day, I know it. If I don't practice for two days, the critics know it. And if I don't practice for three days, the public knows it." I've heard this quote attributed to many other musicians, but whoever said it was 100% right.

Those desiring to become professional musicians ought to first reflect on the quality of their relationship with practicing. In fact, to be a professional anything, the relationship to the work is important. Perhaps that's why they call it "practicing law."

MAKING YOUR FAMILY AND ROOTS YOUR CALLINGS

Your calling doesn't have to be sports or music or require any special skill or talent. It might simply be devoting yourself to your family or your cultural roots. Those are my mom's callings.

Judit, my mother, was born in Budapest on April 25, 1947. There's a good reason why her calling revolves around devoting herself to family and her roots. After the 1956 Hungarian Revolution, her father and brother dramatically vanished from Leányfalu from one day to the next, without even saying goodbye. Their window to freedom in the U.S. was very small and they had to move quickly and discreetly.

This left a deep imprint on my mother, only 9 years old at the time. She would make it a priority to keep her family and friends close and connected for the rest of her life. She vowed to be the backbone of her family, the linchpin of its activities. Later she'd commit to establishing various organizations – including dance groups, museums and institutions – celebrating her cultural and familial roots.

Judit was an excellent student, both in terms of her grades and her impeccable behavior. She loved being a teenager in Budapest, with most summers spent in Leányfalu. Judit and her mother eventually emigrated to the U.S. in 1963 as a result of the U.S.'s family reunification immigration policies. Though such a big move was obviously quite jarring to an otherwise happy teenager, she fit in well with her new American surroundings and had some basic English knowledge, which definitely helped.

After finishing high school in New York, she began studying interior design and worked as a junior artist for J.C. Penney. She immersed herself in New York City's vibrant Hungarian community, where she met my father.

My mother stopped working at J.C. Penney when my sister was born in 1971, taking on the traditional stay-at-home role while collaborating with my father on a multitude of cultural initiatives. She helped establish a museum within the Hungarian community of Passaic, New Jersey, which further strengthened her interest in learning about world heritages. This drew her to study human behavior and societies. After taking years of evening classes and studying late nights at the kitchen table, she graduated with a B.A. in Anthropology from Montclair State University in 1985. She wrote her thesis on the Hungarian community of Passaic, an industrial city which attracted many Eastern/Central European immigrants starting in the 1800's.

In a fortunate turn, my mom re-entered the full-time workforce in the travel industry, becoming Sales Director of Malév Hungarian Airlines' New York office. This meant decidedly discounted or even free stand-by flights from 1987 to 1995. I was able to travel widely during those years, visiting Brazil, Italy, Venezuela, France, and much of the United States. Spending a part of almost every summer in Hungary allowed me to deeply connect with my own cultural roots.

These Malév-funded trips were not all about art galleries and continental breakfasts. My trips to the villages of Transylvania were particularly humbling and life altering. Transylvania is a large area with a sizeable Hungarian population that was part of the Austro-Hungarian Empire before World War I and is within today's Romanian borders.

On one occasion when the brutal Romanian dictator Nicolae Ceaușescu was in power, our hosts begged us to whisper when we spoke Hungarian. Speaking anything other than Romanian was a crime. On a later visit, my friend and I slept in a haystack under the stars when we visited a shepherd in the hills around Transylvania's Carpathian Mountains. I am grateful for those experiences just as much as my visit to Vatican City to get a glimpse of the Pope.

Devotion to cultural roots might sustain many generations. For several years every October, I played the Hungarian harvest dance party in remote Albany, Louisiana. Beginning in 1896, Hungarian immigrants began settling in Albany to work as farmers. Over the ensuing decades hundreds of Hungarian families made their way there, even naming their community "Árpádhon" (home of Árpád) in homage to the founder of Hungary. These are third, even fourth generation Hungarians who honored their ancestry annually by reviving their forefathers' agricultural harvest dance traditions. Unfortunately, Hurricane Katrina in 2005 devastated much of the community and it's had a tough time rebuilding its prior glory.

Far away in another Albany – the state capital of New York – I once performed for George Pataki, the state's Governor for 12 years. Soon after he took office, he invited my band to play at the Governor's Mansion in Albany for the celebration of the Hungarian War of Independence of 1848. He is a proud Hungarian and was eager to show off his Hungarian patriotism at this event. Pataki repeatedly proclaimed his profound admiration for freedom fighter Lajos Kossuth, but mangled his pronunciation so poorly that I cringed each time Pataki spoke Kossuth's name. Years later, together with one of his children, Pataki helped launch ReConnect Hungary, a birthright program for young Americans and Canadians with Hungarian heritage to explore their cultural identity. This, for me, makes up for the errant pronounciation I witnessed.

In a fitting nod to their own heritage, my parents now live only a few steps away from where my mom grew up – on the Buda side of the Danube River, across the street from the university where her mom had been a secretary decades ago. And my parents spend much of their summers in Leányfalu. Talk about connecting with your family and cultural roots!

CREATE A LEGACY FOR YOUR CALLING

Once you've identified and pursued your own personal calling, you might also consider ways to generate a legacy in that area. You know that feeling when you're so excited about something you can't sleep? That's what creating a legacy through creating content feels like. The beauty of endless possibilities!

There are two parties in a transaction when it comes to creating content. One party is the creator, actively involved on the giving end, wheels spinning, burning mental calories creating something for others. The receiving party is on the passive end, cozily ingesting and viewing the content. Those primarily receiving content passively tend to be more lethargic and less engaged in the excitement of life. Over-watching the news, Netflix, and simply observing others' creations rather than creating leads to pretty fast burnout, boredom and apathy.

Creating content is much more vibrant, leaves a legacy, gives you something to look forward to and puts you in life's driver's seat – even though it's more demanding.

Most anyone, for little to no money, can author a book, make a YouTube video, record interviews, publish a blog, post on Twitter, write articles. Find three people to follow your content. First create the content, then the audience. Even if you don't get beyond the audience of three, you're still actively creating content, not just passively absorbing it.

My calling is making music. Most of my content creation in life has been musical – performing, recording, teaching. During the COVID-19 pandemic, all of that came to a halt, and my music-related content creation was down to zero. A string of fully-booked weekends turned to months of time-on-hand.

I decided to create my own personal podcast-type content during the pandemic. I clicked on Facebook Live and started playing some Hungarian folk music and telling stories about my past gigs and adventures. At first I felt it wasn't even good, but my few friends who watched it liked it, and I made more episodes. I added to the content, preparing and delivering some educational material as well.

This attempt to create content during free time was the kernel of what's now "Tanchaz Talk," the world's only English-language program focusing primarily on Hungarian folk music. Episodes are now regularly posted on YouTube and the program's website. I even learned how to put the interviews in podcast form. Best of all, I did all of this for a grand total of zero dollars. No overhead costs.

Worried about where to begin? Don't be. Just start hammering away. Initiate with one word, one paragraph, one clip, one Facebook Live video. Just keep pursuing your calling by creating content and leaving a legacy.

SHARE YOUR TALENTS

Don't hold back from sharing your calling, particularly if it's in the form of some kind of talent.

Back in ancient times, the word "talent" was a unit of weight associated with currency. There's a famous parable in the New Testament about talents. Before a landowner goes away on a trip, he gives some talents to three of his servants. The two servants who made wise investments with the talents and generated profit with them were considered to be faithful and rewarded. The third servant played it safe, burying what he was given in a hole in the ground to protect it. This servant was viewed to be unfaithful and punished by the landowner.

There are a few interpretations of the parable's meaning. Your financial advisor will interpret that parable to make sure you invest money with her. I prefer a more popular interpretation through which the meaning of the word "talent" actually came to mean "skill" or "gift." That interpretation underscores that we are each given talents and we are supposed to put them to use. If we don't use them or share them, we're just hoarding them and digging our gifts into the ground for no good reason. It's a punishable offense, at least according to the landowner in the story. Don't bury your talents.

One of the skills or gifts everybody shares is the ability to come up with new and creative ideas. Some are better at this than others, but we all have had good ideas at one point. Because generating ideas is part of everyone's talent stack, they serve as a simple example of shareable talents. If you have an idea to improve your family, community, workplace – don't hoard it, unload it! Consider getting started by volunteering your time in a local organization or community board. They're always hiring.

No one is above sharing their talents. André Erdős is a former Hungarian Ambassador to the United Nations, probably the highest post for any diplomat. While serving as Ambassador he lived at the Hungarian Consulate in New York, where I was often invited to play music. André liked our music and asked to sit in on the drums one night during some fancy reception. I wasn't sure what to expect but he was great and his sitting in with us became a regular occurrence. His appearances delighted all of the other U.N. diplomats who weren't used to one of their own sharing musical talents so publicly, particularly in such stuffy settings as diplomatic receptions.

Levente Székely, Hungary's former Ambassador-rank representative to Taiwan, is an excellent folk violinist. He played in the band of the Hungarian State Folk Ensemble back in the 1980's. When stationed in Taiwan, he and his wife, a former professional folk dancer, utilized their performing skills to deeply connect with the Taiwanese people. When the Hungarian delegation hosted receptions, Levente played, his wife danced, and the audiences ate it up. Levente says his "musical diplomacy" was a key accomplishment in his career and the best way of showcasing Hungary around the world.

André and Levente's openness for sharing their music so openly was undoubtedly a decisive factor in their career trajectories. The fact they were willing to play, even in unlikely settings, left a positive imprint on those that heard and saw them.

TALES FROM THE OPERA AND THE GOLF COURSE

In January 1996 my parents attended an opera premier at the Metropolitan Opera House. The opera was written by a Czech composer, Leos Janacek. They had two extra tickets and invited another couple, recent immigrants from Hungary who had never been to the opera. A *New York Times* article explains the shocking scene that unfolded:

A 63-year-old tenor with the Metropolitan Opera died last night after apparently suffering a heart attack and falling to the stage from a ladder during the first few minutes of the Met premiere of "The Makropulos Case," by Leos Janacek.

The tenor, Richard Versalle, who was singing the role of Vitek, an elderly clerk in a law firm, had just finished reaching up to a high B and then a B flat as he sang about a legal case that was nearly a century old. As he mounted a sliding ladder to place the file for the case back in its drawer, singing the words "Too bad you can only live so long," his voice faltered and he fell 10 feet from the ladder to the floor, landing on his back with his arms outstretched.

As audience members gasped and cried out, the conductor, David Robertson, yelled repeatedly across the footlights, "Richard, are you all right?" Mr. Versalle was apparently unconscious, and the curtains were immediately brought down as people rushed to the tenor's side.

A spokesman for the Metropolitan Opera, David Reuben, said Mr. Versalle was taken to St. Luke's-Roosevelt Hospital, where he was declared dead shortly after arrival.

It was quite the jarring introduction to opera for my parents' friends. I'm not sure they ever returned to the Met.

My friend Mike Harrington was a life-long golfer and had won many tournaments, including the Ontario Senior Men's Championship, semi-pro club tournaments, and a fair bit of money in friendly bets and side-wagers. His daughter was my wife's best childhood friend, and when we moved to Toronto, Mike routinely invited me to go golfing. I warned him in advance that I liked golf but was not a good golfer; he took me under his wing nonetheless.

Mike turned out to be an absolute whiz at giving personalized instruction ("you know how to dance, just swing those hips like you're dancing") and I enjoyed our many outings at local Toronto courses. But my favorite part of playing with Mike was witnessing his mastery of the game, his strategic attack of each hole, the consistency and fluidity of his swing, all with the bonus of being wildly entertained by the stories of his exploits centered around golf. Mike's calling was golf, no doubt about it – even in his early 80's, he would climb the roof of his winter residence perched along one of the holes of a Florida golf course and collect balls that golfers roughly as gifted as me had shanked all the way to the top of his house. Mike would never let a golf ball go to waste.

A few years ago, at the age of 86, Mike was out for a round of golf with some buddies. Always a gentleman, Mike let the others hit off the tee first as he stood far behind them surveying the fairway, no doubt plotting his next move. "Mike, it's your shot" one of his friends said. He didn't respond. "Mike?" They turned around and saw Mike on the ground, dead from a sudden heart attack. Mike died doing exactly what he loved to do, and I can think of no better way he could have left us – engaged in his calling.

Mark Twain's words at the beginning of this chapter underscore the need to discover a calling. The day you do is as important as the day you were born.

Find your calling, share it, and pursue it before it's too late. None of us will live forever.

PRINCIPLE #4
BE POLITE, PLEASANT AND KIND

"Be kind whenever possible. It is always possible." - Dalai Lama

Parenting three children has taught me that when encouraging positive behavior, it's more effective to explain to a child what she should do instead of what she shouldn't. Before I had kids, an experienced parent explained it this way: Rather than telling a child to not touch a flower (so as not to ruin the flower or break the vase), show the child how to cautiously approach the flower, smell it and delicately feel it. In other words, rather than "don't do that," we should focus on "do it this way." It's positive behavior encouragement. Sounds like a bit of a crunchy granola approach, but it has worked.

The key positive behaviors that would make the world a better place: being polite, pleasant and kind (PPK). Rather than admonish on how not to behave, let's hone in on what it takes to be PPK. Simple examples of PPK behaviors:

• Say thank you

• Greet people (good morning, good afternoon, good evening, hello, goodbye)

• Hold a door open for someone behind you

• Smile, or at least have a content resting face

- Pick up your dog's poop

- Throw garbage out in the garbage can

- If you're able, offer your seat to the elderly, pregnant, disabled or injured

Any given day, we are likely to see many transgressions of these basic acts of PPK. Do you see them? Consider what a wonderful world we would live in if this wasn't the case. You'll never live zestfully unless you commit to consistently being PPK.

GENERATE LOVE AND FORGIVENESS IN LIFELONG RELATIONSHIPS

Being PPK is not easy. It's particularly challenging in our relationships. My parents have been married for over 50 years. Here's their story.

In the 1960's, New York City was descending into a sea of drugs, homicide and homelessness. But it was still the capital of the world and my parents were both studying and living there before they met.

My dad's parents had already started seeking weekend refuge from the City in the tiny community of Highland Lakes, New Jersey, an hour's drive from Manhattan. They saved enough to purchase a modest cottage on a small lake with a dock for a small red rowboat.

In a nod to the family's agricultural heritage, my grandparents called it the "Tanya" which means "farm" in Hungarian. It was definitely not a farm. Growing up, I spent hours in that red rowboat, quietly rowing myself around the tranquil lake.

My ravishing brunette mom had many suitors, but her favorite was my dad. He was the best dancer in their "Hungária" dance group, the life of the party, the center of attention. The Tanya's backyard was just big enough to host my parents' wedding reception in July 1969. It was the summer of Woodstock and the Moon Landing, and their rollicking reception did not disappoint. A few of the attendees – including my parents – ended up fully clothed in the lake by the end of the party.

My parents decided to move full-time to the Tanya soon after their wedding. Highland Lakes hasn't changed much since the summer of '69. My Godmother, the ever-vibrant Sári Sütöri, still lives there and has had a long relationship with the town. A distant cousin of my dad from Kiskunhalas, she was unofficially adopted by my grandparents when she emigrated to the U.S. as a teenager. Sári loyally stayed by their side and embraced Highland Lakes as her lifelong home, drawn to its landscape, wildlife and peacefulness.

When pressed to give away the secret recipe to such a sustained relationship like theirs, my parents usually say it's a combination of unconditional love and the power of forgiveness. These are potent acts of PPK we should remember in life's most special and blessed relationships like marriage.

BE PPK ON THE WWW

In today's online world, the importance of maintaining PPK communication plays an ever-increasing role. In the countless number of lawsuits I've worked on over my career, I've seen how silly social media posts are contorted years later to shed a negative light on the poster despite every good intention. I have also seen too many examples of how internal company correspondences are later used to bite their authors, or even their recipients, in the butt. This includes the use of inappropriate language, conveying incorrect information, or making off-color comments.

To help battle this pattern, I frequently deliver "responsible business communication" training to corporate employees and executives as well as my university students. Presentations focus on underscoring that everything sent or posted remains on the internet and there's some record of it somewhere, forever. People are reminded to ask these questions before pressing "send," "enter" or "post":

• Would I be proud of this message and stand behind it if it appeared on the front page of the *New York Times*?

• If writing about another person, what would they think of my message if they saw it? Would I be well-pleased to show it to them?

• If conveying an opinion in my message, can I defend it with facts or evidence if challenged? Would the opinion stand the test of time? Am I making it clear this is merely opinion rather than fact?

• What would my mom, grandmother, school principal, or a future boss think if they saw the message, picture, image, or video?

It's true that one can still become President of the U.S. while seemingly ignoring this advice (you know who I'm talking about). Also feel free to ignore this advice if you want to be a reality television star.

But such immunity is not available to everyone. The rest of us need to remember that anything that goes online stays there forever and might later be used against us. However, if we ask the above questions before sending or posting anything, that's probably never going to pose a problem.

SIBLING RELATIONSHIPS AS PPK TESTING GROUNDS

Sibling relationships usually serve as solid testing grounds for trying to maintain consistent PPK behavior. My sister, Ildiko, was born in December 1971. From a young age she was outgoing and exhibited a gift for talking a great deal. Two years her junior, I was shy and reserved. She therefore became my unofficial spokesperson. Ildiko was an expert at finishing my sentences, which should not come as a surprise as we did practically every activity together while growing up.

We started playing violin at the same time. Our first public performances were playing duos and we ended up becoming known as the "Magyar Fiddlers." It wasn't always smooth. She hit me in the head with a violin bow once while arguing about dynamics in a piece we were practicing together. The bow broke in half.

Ildiko has always been a terrific violinist. We attended the same schools and extracurricular programs. We formed musical groups together. We went to the same university. She even married one of my best friends.

Ildiko is a confident, self-assured woman, reminiscent of my grandmother Sarolta. After graduating from Duquesne University, she received an M.D. degree from Semmelweis University in Budapest, named after the 19th century doctor who discovered the wonders of washing hands as a way to stop the spread of infection. Since then, Ildiko has put together a very impressive career in the pharmaceutical industry.

I am lucky to enjoy an excellent relationship with Ildiko. Luis Enrique, former soccer player and coach, humorously noted during the pandemic that playing soccer matches behind closed doors without fans was "sadder than dancing with your sister." Well – sorry Coach Luis – my sister and I danced together plenty.

A BAD START

I constantly fail at being PPK. We're all guilty of being impolite, unpleasant, or unkind. I have a real doozy to share from my childhood.

I was born on November 26, 1973 in Boonton, New Jersey. There wasn't much debate that I'd be named the fifth Kalman, although the first to not use the long marks on each letter "a", a nightmare for the local town clerks in New Jersey to process. According to Hungarian tradition, I was nicknamed "Öcsi," or "little brother." My last name, Magyar, literally means "Hungarian." Somebody up my family tree was definitely overcompensating with that choice.

At the time of my birth we were living in Highland Lakes. I was only a few months old when my parents decided to relocate closer to an urban center. We moved to a small starter home in Bogota, New Jersey. Bogota is one of the most densely populated towns in the most densely populated state, with roughly 8,000 people living within less than a square mile. Its popularity is driven by its proximity to Manhattan, about five miles away on Interstate 80.

Hungarian was my first language. It's all we spoke at home. My parents had very few non-Hungarian friends. I didn't even speak English until attending nursery school in Bogota. My primary exposure to the language had been from Mr. Rogers, Sesame Street and Electric Company. I was so reservedly quiet that my teachers thought I had a learning deficiency. And when I did finally start to speak English, a speech therapist in kindergarten had to help me with proper pronunciation of the letters "s" and "z" among others.

Immediately adjacent to Bogota is the oddly-named Teaneck, the first town in the U.S. to voluntarily integrate its schools in the 1960's. Bogota's racial makeup was primarily white, whereas Teaneck was much more diverse. My father's parents had lived in Teaneck for years in a house that was becoming too large for them. They were downsizing and moving full-time to Highland Lakes. My parents bought my grandparents' Teaneck house and we moved in.

I was entering the third grade when we relocated the two miles over to Teaneck. I cried in fear the night before my first day of school, not knowing anyone in my new class. Things got off to a rocky start when playing kickball one day after school, an African-American classmate intentionally kicked the ball onto the roof and I yelled, "Nice kick," followed by the "n" word.

Yup, that "n" word.

This was one of those moments in life when the music stops, you hear the record-scratch noise and everyone stares at you.

I didn't get it – my new classmates were calling each other by that name, so why couldn't I? Besides, I didn't know at the time that it was offensive. Both excuses of ignorance rightfully fell on unsympathetic ears. It was inexcusable, and definitely not PPK. My newly-found Teaneck friends followed me home that day. During the entire walk they repeatedly reminded me that only racists used that word and unambiguously shared their collective conclusion that ergo I must be a racist. I was petrified and pretty much had to talk my way out of a serious ass-kicking, a desperate but early sign of my advocacy skills. It was a mortifying experience for everyone involved, one I will never forget.

It took some time but I eventually patched things up with my friends. By the time Rosa Parks, a hero of the civil rights movement, came to visit our school a few years later, I was thankfully back in the good graces of my classmates. They came to understand I was PPK, not KKK.

Teaneck was propelled into the national spotlight in 1990 when Phillip Pannell, an African-American classmate of mine who was there at the kickball fiasco, was shot dead by a white police officer in an encounter gone bad in a local park. It was no secret that Phillip had a troubled childhood and I remember some negative encounters with Phillip bullying me, sticking his finger in my face. But the shooting was tragic and led to an outcry about racial profiling and police brutality, with protest marches and rioting. Reverends Al Sharpton and Jesse Jackson visited our school in a nationally televised assembly. Racial tension filled the air, which was sad given Teaneck's positive racial history – excluding my kickball incident, of course.

PPK DOESN'T MEAN WEAK

Despite my serious transgressions, I try to do my best to ask whether my contemplated actions or the words I'm about to write or speak are PPK. This is a dicey topic when it comes to lawyers, as the general public seems to mistakenly celebrate lawyers who appear to be the bullying, standoffish and constantly-interrupting "as seen on TV" attorneys.

The legal profession might be the most poorly depicted profession on TV and in films when compared to reality. Actual lawyers are mostly civil to each other, belligerence has no place, and the court system moves at a glacial pace.

Even aggressively-titled books only attorneys read, such as David Berg's *The Trial Lawyer: What It Takes To Win*, teach: "You can't prevail with tender sensibilities. But better to do it sotto voce [with a quiet voice] than bellowing, better by persuasion than bludgeoning. That's the way to win a trial."

I've seen no evidence that rude and mean lawyers negotiate more favorable deals or obtain higher judgments for their clients than PPK ones. You can still be PPK while being a winner, a strong leader, accomplished in your field, a ruthless competitor, confident, a champion, financially wealthy, principled, firm, and someone who stands up to aggressors.

Nice guys might still finish last, but never because they are nice. Only a fool would mistake someone who is being PPK for someone who is weak.

You may or may not achieve what you want, but it is always possible to be polite, pleasant and kind. The Dalai Lama says so, and so do I.

PRINCIPLE #5
HONOR YOUR WORD

"No one cares how much you know, until they know how much you care." - Theodore Roosevelt

Honoring one's word by keeping promises is a concept that might be found in every self-help book ever written. But the number of times this is ignored is simply flabbergasting.

When you promise you'll be somewhere at a specific time, be there. When you promise you'll turn in a project on a certain day, do it. When you promise to call someone back, call. It's that simple. You can never live zestfully if you don't honor your word.

RECOGNIZE THE IMPLIED PROMISE OF RESPONSIVENESS

I believe every relationship we have or want to have comes with an "implied" promise of responsiveness. Existing and prospective clients, colleagues and customers don't give a damn about your knowledge until you show that you can treat them right. Family members and friends won't value you if you keep blowing them off.

Talk is cheap. Just saying "I care about you and your business" is meaningless. We can't show others how much we care by simply saying it. In my experience, there is one compelling, decisive way to show clients and customers how much you care. It's shockingly easy to do.

Don't leave them hanging. Call or write people back immediately. I can virtually guarantee that if you do this you'll be gainfully employed or employable. You'll also enjoy positive relationships with family and friends. This principle applies to everyone, from owners to employees to students. We are all in sales and we all have customers. As PayPal founder Peter Thiel writes in *Zero to One*, "Look around. If you don't see any salespeople, you're the salesperson."

GET INTO THE IMMEDIATE RESPONSE BUSINESS

Given how easy calling or writing people back sounds, it's profoundly disappointing to discover how often it's not done particularly in the business world. There are many highly skilled and knowledgeable people in the marketplace. It's reassuring to know that you can distinguish yourself from the pack by simply adhering to the policy of not leaving anyone hanging.

I've been on both sides of this relationship. Back when I was an in-house lawyer, the outside counsel I best enjoyed working with were not necessarily the ones who had the highest IQ or stellar experience. The ones I adored were those that called and wrote me back immediately. Even if they couldn't deal with me right away, a simple "got it, will get back to you" made me feel acknowledged. Sure, being wined and dined was a nice touch too, but nothing beats that immediate response time.

Now in private practice, I know that my law firm is just one of the thousands out there. We're never going to be able to differentiate ourselves by being the most knowledgeable, though we might very well be. Instead, I find comfort in redefining our mission.

Rather than simply being in the legal business, I like to think that we're also in the immediate response business. Just as you shouldn't underestimate people's capacity to be lazy or irresponsible, take solace in knowing that many people fail at the immediate response model. Adopting immediate responsiveness as a core part of your business' DNA is a definitive competitive edge.

You will hear extreme guidance from people who recommend blocking out time once or twice a week only for responding to emails. Unless you enjoy some special form of monopoly or you are well-off and secure enough to not immediately respond to clients, customers or colleagues, I think you should ignore that advice. It reminds me of the rabbit busily hopping around the forest who sees an eagle sitting high up in a tree doing absolutely nothing. The exhausted rabbit asks, "Can I do that too?" "Sure thing," the eagle responds. The rabbit sits on the ground under the tree, when a fox suddenly appears and eats the rabbit as the eagle looks on. The moral of the story: To be sitting and doing nothing, you must be sitting very, very high up.

Response time might be the easiest metric to measure after pure profit-loss. This holds true whether you're a plumber, baker, youth sports coach, or anything else. And it secretly might have the most direct impact on your bottom line and job performance.

Some of my most loyal clients are those I have lost big with. They stick by me even after we go through tough times together. This tells me that the result is often less important than the attention you give clients in the process of getting to that result.

THE BROKEN PROMISE THAT CAN'T BE ERASED

When I was a junior in university, I scurried off to the local Emergency Room after banging my head against a fence while playing pick-up soccer. During the intake examination the E.R. doctor observed something strange in my right ear. She asked whether I had stuck something in my ear. "Never," I replied. She kept asking, "Are you sure?" I was adamant, "Yes I'm sure," confident it's something I wouldn't forget.

A week later I had some stitches in my head but I was now at the ENT specialist as a result of the ear examination. He sat me in the chair, took a look, and said that I definitely had something stuck in there. He inserted a giant needle in my right ear. While we were waiting for the ear to numb, he asked me if I wanted to keep whatever he took out. "Definitely," I asserted. What a keepsake!

After a few minutes, he started going to town on my ear with various contraptions. He showed me what he eventually extracted – an eraser from the tip of a pencil. It's still a mystery how that eraser became lodged in my ear. When I was younger, I probably was picking at my ear with a pencil and the eraser fell off and got stuck. Had I noticed, I probably would have told my parents. But the eraser was in my ear for at least five years, maybe more.

The doctor didn't let me keep the eraser. He left the room with it and never came back. No doubt he added it to his weird collection of other items retrieved from patients' ears – toys, marbles, beans, and who knows what else. The point is, he broke his promise. And you can't erase that broken promise.

EMPTY YOUR INBOX

This advice is very "micro" and specific, but it has been decisive in terms of staying responsive to my clients. It also enables me to approach my work with energy and a clear head.

It's this: I do my best to keep my email inbox empty. That's not hyperbole. Empty, as in zero.

Keeping a clean workspace has historically meant carefully organizing files and folders and having a clutter-free desk. Those days are now gone, as we focus on reducing paper altogether and organizing our lives electronically. I don't want to date myself too much, but my first personal email address during university and law school was something like "784209@compuserve.com." We've come a long way.

As a business lawyer, emails are now my key form of daily communication. And when it comes to emails, having them in my inbox equals desk clutter. I actually have trouble going to sleep if there's something in my inbox – whether in my work

(Outlook) or my personal (Yahoo) accounts. I'll miss messages and opportunities unless I clear the clutter.

Maintaining my "inbox zero" status only works in tandem with a strategically developed To-Do List, an Excel spreadsheet which groups together my tasks in 3 categories based on priority as follows:

• Group 1 = on-the-go, working on it actively (sometimes I'll bold one of these tasks and put it on top of the list when it's really urgent)

• Group 2 = keep an eye on this task; either waiting for someone to get back to me on it, or kind of a back-burner project

• Group 3 = not important or active at all but something I cannot forget about

Once I complete a task, I might delete or move it from a "1" to a "3" so I can cut-and-paste as needed. The List has 3 columns – Column A (showing if the task belongs in Group 1, 2 or 3); Column B (name of matter, client, issue); and Column C (more detailed description of the task). My To-Do List spreadsheet is open all-day and is my BFB (best friend in business).

Now back to the emails. When receiving an email, I generally have three options:

• If I can deal with it right away, I'll respond and move the email from the Inbox and my response from the Sent folder into a subfolder relating to that matter

• If it's something I want to take my time responding to, I start drafting an email but close it (saving into Drafts) and move the email from the Inbox into the appropriate subfolder

• If it's something that requires more work, I move the email into the proper folder, and update my To-Do List reflecting that I need to respond to that email

I also always clear my Sent folder – either by deleting or moving sent emails into its relevant folder.

My stress level decreases as I move workflow away from my direct line of sight. In essence, I am telling my workflow, "I see you, I hear you, and I will deal with you when I can" without the constant reminder of seeing emails in my inbox.

I know this might not work for everyone, but it has worked wonders for me. While my process may sound rigid, I find it liberating to work in an environment where my inbox is empty. And it makes space for responding immediately.

DEVELOP PROMISE-KEEPING PRACTICES

My weekends growing up were filled with full-on heritage immersion. A similar drill was playing out for many first-generation Hungarian immigrant kids from Long Island to Los Angeles and from Sydney to Buenos Aires. Friday nights meant folkdance practice. Saturdays featured language school in the morning and Hungarian Scouts in the afternoon. Sundays involved serving as an altar boy for Roman Catholic mass at the Hungarian Church, with lengthy homilies reminding us about the evils of communism and demanding the re-annexation of Transylvania. After Mass, there was usually a community luncheon, bake sale or cultural commemoration.

This was all before the invention of electronic gaming and we kept ourselves entertained while avoiding our elders' looming eyes. They wouldn't hesitate to slap us upside the face if we did something stupid. Those were different times. It was back when "go to your room" was intended as a punishment.

In other respects, I was a bit of a black sheep in the Hungarian community despite being involved in all of these activities. This is because they were all secondary to my music studies.

Thanks to good research and some solid choices by my parents, I had an intense music education. It laid the groundwork for everything good that followed in my life, including my university experience, finding jobs as a young lawyer, meeting my wife and pursuing my calling in music.

I began taking violin lessons at the age of five from Erika Boyd, a warm-hearted and amiable teacher in Leonia, New Jersey through the "Suzuki" method, named after the Japanese pedagogue Shinichi Suzuki with whom Boyd had studied directly. The method emphasizes looking, listening and imitating, in contrast to traditional reading-based systems. This turned out to be the optimal choice for a future folk musician. Ms. Boyd's group classes were filled with mostly Japanese kids and just a few European immigrant families like ours. The Suzuki method is more mainstream today.

When I was nine years old, Ms. Boyd recommended my sister and I take the next step in our development and apply to the Preparatory Division of Manhattan School of Music (MSM). MSM, located in East Harlem, is an audition-only all-day Saturday program for pre-college music students. We auditioned and were accepted. I took not just classical violin and viola but theory, ear training, composition, choir, jazz ensemble, and chamber music. The highlight was playing in the symphonic orchestra. It was truly high-brow stuff.

We both studied with Stanley Bednar, formerly a wunderkind virtuoso who transitioned into teaching and served as an MSM faculty member since 1954. True to his generation, he was a chain smoker and his cigarette would dangle from his mouth while he made adjustments to my positioning, bits of ash falling on the violin's fingerboard. He was critical but kind, stressing proper technique and tone. He cared little about repertoire, promoting etudes and scales instead.

While my peers were rotating through the Paganini and Tchaikovsky concerto treadmill, Mr. Bednar was methodically harping on sound, posture, bow-hand execution and musicality. It took patience but this ended up being a terrific long-term strategy for me as I would continue to play music all my life. Repertoire without technique is as useful as a bitcoin salesman in 1960.

I am fortunate to have been taught by Ms. Boyd and Mr. Bednar, who made me the musician I am today. Both have passed away but I will never forget them.

My music school was once a week on Saturdays. The other days I was in "regular" school where I was no angel. My grades were fine but it took a while for my behavior to match them. My parents kept a collection of notes from teachers which include these:

• 2nd Grade: "Kalman is a fine student. He writes creative stories and has a lot to offer the class. He tends to be mischievous."

• 4th Grade: "Kalman is an excellent student with fine abilities. It is very important, however, that Kalman focus on the academic activities of each day instead of looking for ways to socialize."

• 5th Grade: "Kalman could learn to be a better listener – he need not do most of the talking in class."

• 8th Grade: "Kalman calls out and wise cracks constantly. Has trouble understanding proper procedure for class participation and teacher's role as focus of attention. Kalman should learn to participate without interrupting the flow of the lesson or the other students' attention."

I should have respected my non-music teachers more. Still, in my defense, there was a peculiar write-up from my 2nd grade teacher who simply misunderstood my intentions. I was showing my classmates how to properly perform the Hungarian bottle dance, but this is what the note explained to my mom: "Dear Mrs. Magyar: This afternoon the teacher on duty outside reported on five of the children & mentioned a few others. She specifically mentioned Kalman who she said was putting his bottle on the cement and jumping over it. He also was waving it in another boy's face. I suggest that he use a thermos instead of a glass bottle – and that a word from you about behaving in line might help." I guess this teacher never took the "Intro to Hungarian Folkdance" class.

In 1987, while studying at the MSM and slogging through Teaneck's school system, my sister and I had formed our first folk music band, Életfa. We were barely teenagers. Just two years before, we had wanted to quit playing music altogether to focus on sports instead. Our parents held tough, basically saying, "Good talk, now go downstairs and keep practicing." Thank goodness they didn't give in.

Életfa was the first band in North America focused solely in the repertoire of the "Táncház," a phenomenon which took off in Budapest during the 1970's and was gaining popularity in North America by the 1980's. "Táncház" literally means "dance house" and is the focal point of the revival of Hungarian music and dance in their purest form. It quickly became the go-to band for Hungarian folkdance events all over the U.S. and Canada, from dank Church halls to big-league concert halls.

The famous actor Alec Baldwin once narrated a performance at Lincoln Center where Életfa played in collaboration with the New York Philharmonic Orchestra. Backstage he saw my sister decked out in her ethnic costume, slowly approached her, and in deliberate, measured English to make sure she understood, asked, "Where. Are. You. From?" My sister quickly replied in her perfect American accent, "New Jersey." Outraged that she wasn't exotically ethnic enough for what he was expecting, Baldwin walked away disgusted.

I still remember sitting in our living room in Teaneck when we came up with the band's name. The translation for Életfa is "tree of life" and was perfect for what the band has achieved. True to its name, since its beginning (roots) the group has gone through various iterations (branches) over time, as musicians eventually moved away from the New York area and others joined. The group is still alive today.

Parallel to our musical ventures, my sister and I kept dancing with the "Hungária" folkdance group, which had moved its practice location from New York to New Jersey. We were the group's second generation and, like for our parents, it served as the focal point of the members' social lives. It's actually mind-boggling to consider how much time we all spent together. Aside from the long practices and many performances, we hung out at parties, went to the movies, visited theme parks, and did whatever else teenagers did together in the 1980's and early 1990's.

Keeping up with all of these parallel pursuits was not easy. It entailed making promises on multiple fronts – music, dance, school – and keeping them.

But there was a greater purpose that revealed itself when, on a rare free weekend night during high school, my parents took my sister and me to see the Duquesne University Tamburitzans on tour in New Jersey. We didn't know too much about the group and had never spoken about it growing up. I was surprised to discover that the 40-member group established in 1937 was the longest-running multicultural music and dance company in the U.S. The members were full-time students at Pittsburgh's Duquesne University who received full scholarships in exchange for performing every weekend and during extended school holidays. This was like playing NCAA Division I ball, except it was year-round with over 100 shows annually.

In July the group gathered for a three-week training camp during which a new two-hour show was assembled, featuring Central/East European folk repertoire stretching from Poland to Turkey. They began touring in August, then moved into the dormitories and began classes at Duquesne. The students' area of study ran the gamut from pharmacy to philosophy. Very few were music majors.

Every Friday afternoon the students would hop into a customized bus and perform at venues throughout the country. The students studied and slept on the bus and were back in time for Monday morning classes. During school holidays and breaks they'd go on longer trips with shows at Disney World, up and down the west coast, even Las Vegas. There was a break in June and then back to the camp in July to create an entirely new show for the year.

My mind was blown when I saw the Tamburitzans on stage that first night. Their show was highly professional, tasteful and mightily entertaining. It promised the coolest possible university experience. We got a chance to look inside the tour bus which was awesome in itself.

All the years of balancing music, dance and school activities made sense – the Tamburitzans could serve as our ticket to a free education as we continued to share our heritage. My sister auditioned and was accepted in 1990. By that point, I was also ready to hop on that Tamburitzans' bus, but I was only in 10th grade. But there was a way I could graduate high school early. During my junior year (11th grade), I took the required English course at Bergen Community College and History at Montclair State University. Both classes were filled with adults, and I had to explain my pimply presence to older classmates multiple times – I was there to skip my last year in high school and I needed to take these two classes to make this happen.

Together with these courses and my many MSM extra credits, I finished high school in three years. Graduating after my junior year meant no prom, no yearbook picture, no senior send-off. But I was itching to move on to the next stage of my scholastic and performing life, and because I was so immersed within my Hungarian community, I never got around to creating a social circle within my high school. I didn't feel like I was losing much by leaving.

I was accepted for admission to Duquesne, auditioned for the Tamburitzans, and was offered a full scholarship in 1991. I didn't bother applying to any other university. What followed was a four-year master class in promise keeping and time management. We were living the motto that the busier you are, the more you seem to get done. Looking at my fellow Tamburitzan colleagues, it was clear that they were all adept at keeping promises. To get to that level in the performing arts as a student they had to be. It was a part of their core values.

The enduring memories from those years are not necessarily connected to the nearly 500 shows we played. Rather, I most relish the opportunities to see the U.S. and appreciate its vastness and beauty: the majestic Grand Canyon, vibrant Harvard Square, San Antonio's canals, unmatchable Wyoming, cliffs of La Jolla, presidents of Mount Rushmore, jazz in New Orleans, chowder at Fisherman's Wharf.

Though the members of the Tamburitzans were on the road every Friday afternoon to Monday morning, most of them were on the Dean's List. I graduated from Duquesne's business school with a cum laude degree in accounting in 1995. I'll forever cherish the experiences and friendships of those four years, which would not have been possible without my somewhat unique and bustling upbringing.

GETTING ADDICTED TO HONORING YOUR WORD

The funny thing about keeping your promises is that once you're used to doing it with respect to others, you can start making promises to yourself. You become so hooked on keeping promises that you'll be hard-pressed to break them. For instance, if you promise yourself to go jogging at a specific time on a specific day, you will be bound to keep that promise. You'll feel like crap for breaking your self-promise. This is why I rarely make such sweeping exercise-related self-promises.

Honor your word, honor yourself. Take your promises seriously and do your best to keep them. Doing so creates a steamroll effect and breeds new and exciting opportunities to make and keep other promises. It's one of the most well-known but often-ignored principles of a zestful life.

PRINCIPLE #6
EMBRACE REJECTION

"Success is buried on the other side of rejection." - Tony Robbins

If you're engaged in the game of life to its fullest, the times you are rejected will far outnumber your acceptances. Fortunately – yes, fortunately – I've been rejected many more times than I've been accepted. I use the word "fortunately" here by design because most of these rejections have been for good reasons, though I didn't appreciate them at the time. Here are just three examples.

In 2004, I was invited to audition for Cirque du Soleil, which was looking for a violinist with an "ethnic" flair. It would have been an amazing experience to join the company, at least for a few years, with my legal degree to fall back on. I was well prepared and felt that I performed well for the panel of musical scouts that had assembled in a musty New York studio for their traveling audition road show. But they didn't accept me, explaining they were looking for someone "different."

Now I appreciate that while I'm working as a lawyer, I'm unlikely to land a musical job like this, no matter how qualified I am. These full-time, almost corporate-type jobs are rightfully reserved for candidates who don't have law degrees to fall back on and are 100% devoted to their craft. And, of course, those with an intimate relationship with practicing I never had.

Later I was considering starting my own law firm in New Jersey but didn't have any of my own clients. I needed some guaranteed income flow and medical benefits for my family to get things going. Our local Roman Catholic Church was hiring for a part-time music director with benefits, which would've been an optimal solution. While the pastor liked my style, he felt the choir needed a director with more "formal" music training, so he hired a woman with a master's degree in music. She turned out to be a bad fit with the choir and the pastor called me a few months later asking if I was still interested in the gig. However, by that time (early 2007), I was hired for my dream legal job in Toronto. Had it not been for the initial rejection, I would never have considered the Toronto position.

I once had a job interview with a big firm partner who asked me off-the-wall questions like "what words start with the letters dw" and a baseball hypothetical about how someone standing on first base can score without the batter hitting the ball or being walked or having a wild pitch thrown (or something like that – I'm still trying to decipher what the question was). This is a technique to try to throw a candidate off and see how he reacts on his feet, but I still think of that guy when I reflect on the fact that there are more horses' asses than horses in the world. He did not make me an offer. In hindsight, I'm happy I didn't get the job because this was clearly not a guy I could work for. I also learned his large firm imploded a few years later, dwindling to nothing.

These are just three examples of why I try to embrace rejection. They are usually part of a bigger plan that will only reveal itself later. Sometimes it becomes clear only years down the line.

"Successful people fail their way to the top" writes Jeff Olson in *The Slight Edge*.

REDUCE THE CHANCE OF REJECTION

During my last year in high school, I made a decision to attend law school after university. My GPA at Duquesne was respectable, but the dreaded Law School Admission Test (LSAT) evens the playing field among applicants from all of the country's disparate universities and colleges. Though it was a test I studied pretty hard for, looking at my results it was humbling to discover I wasn't as smart as I thought I was.

My parents' college graduation gift to me was to pay for application fees to 20 law schools. With my GPA and LSAT score, I knew which schools I'd have a good chance of getting into. But since I had carte-blanche to apply to so many schools, I sent applications to the likes of Harvard, Yale and Columbia, almost as a goof. Obviously these Ivy League schools all rejected me. My fiddle playing could only carry me so far.

I decided to attend Brooklyn Law School, one of the schools that actually accepted me. In 1995 I moved to a small one-bedroom Manhattan apartment overlooking the entrance of the Lincoln Tunnel with Zoran Zgonc, one of my best friends from the Tamburitzans. It was a great three years at 34th Street and 10th Avenue, even though specs of dirt and soot would make their way into our tenth floor apartment through the windows from the cars piled up in unending tunnel traffic right under us.

My law school tuition was funded by low-interest federal government loans which took over a decade to repay. Most of my rent was covered by playing weekend gigs. The apartment was 30 minutes from the law school via subway and was conveniently located for my roommate Zoran who was working at the Late Show with David Letterman. Sometimes he scored a comp ticket for me to Late Show tapings. I got to hear one of my musical heroes, Paul Shaffer, and his band. At one show I sat beside the aisle and Diana Ross kissed me on my cheek as she sang running through the audience.

But on most Friday afternoons, I would walk to Port Authority and take the bus back to my parents' house in Teaneck to use their car to get to gigs. I played a wide mix of folkdance events, weddings, balls and private parties all over the tristate area, reaching a form of "stardom" though only within the limited universe of Hungarian-American musicians – well short of Paul Shaffer and Diana Ross.

While I am a big proponent of enriching the undergraduate experience through a healthy volume of extra-curricular activities or scholarship opportunities like the Tamburitzans, my current advice is the opposite for graduate students. Buckle down, lock yourself in the library, and bust your butt, at least for the first year. I didn't follow this advice. It was a tactical mistake to treat my first year in law school as a continuation of the traveling and touring Tamburitzans days. I took on too many gigs and travelled too much. I didn't put myself in a position to receive top marks.

The initial decade of a legal career is usually dictated by first year law school grades. This is unfortunate and not necessarily predictive of future value in the legal field, but it's the way of the world. Those not at the top of their class after the first year are always forced to devise their own way, a trek replete with rejection. Much has been written about the law school experience. Most of it is true. Brooklyn Law School, New York's largest, had its own particular vibe. The majority of my cohorts were Jewish liberals from Long Island, with some conservative Staten Island Italians sprinkled in. The level of preparation and attention needed to absorb a single class was nothing I ever experienced before.

The method of teaching was, as advertised, mostly based on the Socratic method. Professors would arbitrarily call on students to present cases from the readings. As luck would have it, it seems I was only called upon the days when I wasn't fully prepared. There was no winging it like in university. The roastings we'd receive were dreadful.

One of the aspects I liked most about law school was meeting people of varying ages and life experiences: Avi, the 60-something activist cabdriver; Jodi, the mall rat from Long Island; Steve, who had taught English in Japan; and Jack, the jock who disliked all of them. I ended up finding my tribe of musicians as well, joining the band "Equinox" – great rock musicians who had attended SUNY Binghamton before going to Brooklyn Law School as a pack. We played together for over five years, with many crowded performances in Greenwich Village's Bitter End and Elbow Room, even after our law school run ended.

I should have focused more on studying than gigging my first year of law school. I would have avoided over a decade of rejections. Things worked out eventually, but it just took longer to get there.

DEVISE YOUR OWN OPPORTUNITIES

It's important to have an internship after your first year of any graduate school, even for no compensation. Yet too many students have fallen victim to waiting for paid jobs. If they get rejected or don't get an interview at all, they often sit around all summer and do nothing. That's a mistake. Only the fortunate few – la crème de la crème – will get those calls. The rest of us need to create our own paths, devise our own opportunities, offer to work for free and try to learn whatever and wherever we can.

That's what the summer of 1996 was all about for me.

Professors at Brooklyn Law School were an impressive bunch. There were former district attorneys, constitutional scholars, retired judges, actively practising big-firm lawyers, and Supreme Court clerks. Plenty of them "wrote the book" on whatever subjects they were teaching. One of my professors was Maryellen Fullerton, a leading expert on immigration law who had been a Marshall fellow in Budapest and later became the interim Dean of the law school.

I met Professor Fullerton during my first year and learned that her husband was working as the resident partner of the New York office of a sizeable Hungarian law firm, Nagy & Trócsányi. What a coincidence! As a straight "B-" law student, I was rejected for various well-established summer jobs and knew the phone wouldn't ring on its own with lucrative job offers. The planets were aligning for a post-first year unpaid summer internship.

Nagy & Trócsányi was formed soon after the Iron Curtain collapsed. Its partners had the entrepreneurial spirit that stood in sharp contrast to the stoic way business was done under the communist regime. They quickly rose to become one of Hungary's largest home-grown law firms and in the mid-1990's opened a New York office, the first ever American office of a Hungarian firm. It was comprised of two sublet rooms with a secretarial station within the beautiful Grace Building headquarters of Coudert Brothers, the world's most prominent multinational law firm before it dissolved (due mainly to skyrocketing overhead, like having offices within the beautiful Grace Building).

We worked out a custom-made internship with Nagy & Trócsányi in the summer of 1996. I spent six weeks at the New York office and six weeks in Budapest. It's a good thing I wasn't paid because I was useless at both locations. In New York they had just the one partner and not too much going on. The Budapest office was rip-roaring busy, but my Hungarian legalese was woefully deficient to add any value. I did get to briefly meet named partner László Trócsányi, a constitutional expert who went on to become the Minister of Justice for Viktor Orbán's government and a Member of the European Parliament.

Graduate students should consider offering to work for free at the very start of their careers. There are many Nagy & Trócsányi-esque "jobs" out there, but not if you're waiting for a paycheck.

Devising one's own internship has worked in my musical development as well. Every folk musician knows that the best way to learn folk music, handed down from generation to generation, is to "sit in" with other musicians during live gigs. This usually means inviting yourself – humbly, and for no compensation, no matter how good you might be – to a community dance, party, wedding, or other event, with the intention of soaking in the musical atmosphere, getting a feel for how things go and the style in which the music is played.

It's all about receiving real-time on-site learning which money can't buy and no one should ever pay you for.

PLANT SEEDS OF INTEREST FOR THE FUTURE

Take as many classes as possible in areas that interest you. Even for those long out of school, there are endless amounts of free online educational courses, YouTube tutorials, and other resources available to pursue an interest about a particular subject.

In law school, aside from my required ethics class, the only class in which I ever got an "A" was Food & Drug Law. I even won an award for having the highest grade in the class, from the Center for Computer-Assisted Legal Instruction, which was odd since the class' instruction was not computer-assisted.

Though I would only start to practice food and drug law ten years after that, the seed of interest was planted.

My thirst for food and drug law must have flowed from my dad, who graduated from Long Island University with a B.S. in Chemistry. He started working as a chemist for Purdue Frederick Company before joining the lab at the U.S. Department of Justice in Manhattan, helping test seized drugs for controlled substances. In the 1970's, New Jersey was becoming a pharmaceutical hotbed and my father became a chemist for Sandoz. He transitioned into regulatory roles, eventually rising to an international regulatory affairs and compliance associate director position in the 1990's for Pfizer, in its Grand Central Station headquarters.

Pfizer, one of the world's largest drug companies, has had a prodigious presence in my life. My sister worked for Pfizer as an intern after receiving her medical degree. My cousin, Stephen Vamossy's wife has worked there for almost two decades. Stephen's brother, John, has worked for Pfizer for even longer. My wife worked for Pfizer indirectly, when she trained Pfizer's bubbly salespeople for a New Jersey-based pharmaceutical software company.

In the summer of 1997, between my second and third years of law school, my dad was able to swing a paid internship for me in Pfizer's legal department. The dozen or so legal interns operated in a large room with many cubicles, all students like me writing fruitless memos on esoteric subjects which no lawyer in her right mind would rely on. I quickly learned that they all had parents, relatives or good friends working full-time somewhere in the building.

It was a blur of free lunches, Yankee games, banker's hours, and generous weekly paychecks. Great job for a pretty cool company.

Now I do plenty of work in food and dietary supplement law. I credit Pfizer's summer program experience in guiding me to this practice area. To my chagrin, none of my clients ever ask what grade I received in Food & Drug Law. Too bad, as it marks the pinnacle of my otherwise unremarkable law school career which came to a close in 1998.

THE FEAR OF REJECTION

Law school teaches us how to think, not what to think. That's why the Socratic method is the go-to way of teaching. Only after law school – when studying for bar exams – do we really start down the process of learning what to think.

Bar exams are premised on challenging even the most overachieving students for whom good grades have usually come easy. It strikes the fear of rejection into test takers. That fear breeds months of nonstop studying and over-the-top test preparation.

I should know, as I've gone through the process a few times.

My first set of bar exams was the popular New York-New Jersey combo right out of law school. I treated studying for them like a full-time job. For a few weeks I attended all-day bar prep classes. Based on the lectures and the handouts, I prepared handwritten outlines for every subject. I stared at them in the weeks before the exam, attempting to memorize the material and taking practice exams. Studying the hardest I ever have in my life, I still felt relatively sure I would fail. Bar exams tend to have that effect.

I had to wait about two months until they released the list of results. I tried to "dial in" to the busy server a few times (the internet worked a bit differently then) until I finally saw my name listed just after midnight – "pass"! I celebrated by deliriously running naked into my backyard in Teaneck chased by my wife, then still my girlfriend.

About ten years later, after moving to Toronto, it was time to take the formally-named "Barristers & Solicitors Examinations" for my "call" to the Law Society of Ontario, which was then fancifully named the "Law Society of Upper Canada." With my job at the time being U.S.-focused, I didn't need to take the Ontario examination, but figured it would help cement my standing in Canada.

In the U.S., we are "admitted" to the Bar ("admitted" as into a psychiatric hospital), while in Canada we are "called" to the Bar (as in summoned by court order). Despite all the haughty nomenclature, the Canadian test is easier and the exam is open book, with a high passing rate. More stress is placed on the required 10-month "articling" period, which was waived for me given my prior work experience. I already had three kids and a full-time job when studying for the Ontario exam, but took it seriously, mostly for fear of having to re-write it. "Pass," again.

The most recent bar exam I wrote was in Florida, in February 2019. Why not get admitted in the place I love to escape the dreaded northern winters! I dusted off my old handwritten outlines from 1998 with the material still relevant in many respects, and used some of the apps and online materials I would have loved to have access to two decades before. During the two-day examination in Tampa, I was surrounded mostly by recent law graduates and was one of the old farts. I had sympathy for these super stressed-out youngsters, most of them rewriting the exam, needing to pass to have any chance of getting a decent job. The passing rate was a ghastly 58%, but I passed.

THE ART OF LETTING GO

During my judicial clerkship after law school, I took a one-day training course to become a court-certified mediator. Every clerk had to take turns mediating cases in the small claims court located in the basement of the courthouse. Mandatory mediation sessions run by clerks was a clever way of trying to get rid of these small-stake cases before they went to trial, without any additional burden on taxpayers since we were salaried clerks.

The mediation rotation had me downstairs once every few weeks in the "People's Court" as I called it. We'd be randomly assigned cases and had 30 minutes to try help the parties settle. Neighbors squabbled over landscaping issues. Friends sued each other for unpaid undocumented cash loans. Fender bender car damage, breach of small construction contracts, damages to clothes caused by dry cleaners. You name it, Passaic County Small Claims Court had it all.

The frequent stance of defiance these self-represented litigants had against settling was, "It's about the principle, man." To this, the judge who trained us had a great response. He would say, "principles don't pay." I would use that line once in a while and it actually had the desired effect, leading to some settlements. Some other cases were hopeless. The grudges the parties had against each other were too ingrained to undo.

Grudges are generally idle baggage. If you hold one, you're carrying extra weight for nothing. If someone wrongfully rejected, hurt or did something horrible to you, you don't necessarily have to forgive the bad act. But it's always within your power to forgive the person. One of my father's favorite pictures that still hangs on his office wall is of Pope John Paul II visiting and forgiving the man that tried to assassinate him in 1981.

A prudent resolution of a lawsuit occurs when both sides leave the table disappointed. If a case is about money (and most of them are), in a sensible settlement one side will pay more than they expected to pay and the other side will accept less money than they wanted to accept. That's what makes it a "settlement." If one side leaves the table happy and the other leaves disappointed, that's not really a settlement. It's more of a "win" for the happy side, and a "loss" for the other.

Life is not usually about "winning" or "losing." It's more about "settling" which means letting go of arguments and avoiding situations that create toxicity and negativity in our lives. Remember what the judge said: "Principles don't pay." What pays is making room in your life to follow the principles for zestful living with integrity. Try to steer clear of what might stand in the way of that goal.

Start with letting go of grudges against those that might have rejected you. Embrace them instead.

PRINCIPLE #7
SHOOT STRAIGHT

"From me you shall hear the whole truth...and I do not want any of you to expect anything different." - Socrates

Our society should be built on trust and truth. But it's not. It seems that straight shooters might in fact be a rare breed. Straight shooters are people who:

• speak openly and honestly

• communicate clearly and get to the point quickly

• avoid guessing or predicting without foundation

• are comfortable enough in their own skin to make others look good

Always try to shoot straight.

SPEAK WITH CANDOR

Nothing beats the intellectual high of arguing a case in front of a judge. Trial lawyers live for it – bobbing, weaving, attacking, retreating. The judge I clerked for taught that while he expected lawyers to vigorously advocate for their clients, he also needed assistance in making sure he arrived at fair and just outcomes. He valued lawyers who conceded points that weren't in their clients' favor. The judge could trust these lawyers to help guide his reasoning.

Arguments by straight-shooting lawyers who fess up to flaws in their case carry more weight than those who bombastically fight on every point. This is not only true inside courtrooms but outside them as well. When we acknowledge the elephant in the room, our words land on more receiving, open ears. Conveying an opinion or position – to a colleague, friend, family member – might often have more impact when we do it in a way that implies a concession that "I may be wrong." Because, guess what, we just might be wrong. Humility is strength, not a weakness.

We often hate to say "I don't know" – particularly in the business world. People sometimes count on you to know. If you don't know, they might move on to someone who purportedly does. But candor is more important than waffling or talking gibberish. Rather than admitting "I don't know," I like to say, "I don't know, but I know someone who does." Clients like getting that kind of value. And that means, in addition to working hard to find answers, it's equally important to develop a network of contacts and colleagues to turn to for answers unknown. Our network is an integral part of our added value and a piece of what our clients pay for, no matter the industry or profession. If you can't shoot straight on a particular matter, find someone who can.

DON'T YELL

Communicating clearly does not mean yelling in an effort to be heard.

Arturo Gonzalez, partner of the peerless law firm of Morrison Foerster, is one of the best trial lawyers I've ever worked with. He is the son of Mexican immigrant farmers and graduated from Harvard Law School, an improbable leap from one generation to the next. It's hard to describe Arturo's power until you are in a room with him, but he connects with people in an eerily low-key way. He lets his sense of storytelling and sincerity guide the conversation, rather than the volume of his voice.

Many years ago, with only me at his side as his client representative, Arturo walked into a large federal courtroom in San Francisco armed with just a briefcase. On the other side of the aisle stood more than two dozen lawyers, with paralegals carrying boxes on dollies and hot to trot third-year big firm associates getting their first whiff of a courtroom. One could already hear the other side in this litigation had the volume turned up to eleven. Once the judge came out, Arturo wiped the floor with everyone, always maintaining his soothing, eloquent and tempered tone.

The musical equivalent of Arturo is the illustrious Serbian singer Zvonko Bogdan from Vojvodina. When performing in loud jampacked halls, most musicians tend to turn the volume up in order to be heard through the noise. Zvonko does the opposite. He tells his musicians to back off their mics. He starts to sing almost in a whisper. Instinctively people stop talking and lean in to hear. The most impactful moments of his performances happen with a whisper rather than a bang.

I once saw a violin concert advertised as featuring Klezmer music "played on a violin rescued from the Holocaust." The history of the instrument itself, tragic as it might have been, likely had little impact on the quality of the music performed. But establishing that emotional connection between the audience and the violin played on that night probably gave the listeners an experience they would cherish for a long time.

Rather than focusing on volume or size, try drilling down on substance and furnish a compelling story. It's easy to bribe a crowd into a standing ovation, but it takes true mastery to evoke a gasp from the audience. Remember that you don't have to yell to get a message across. Rumi, the Persian poet, had it right: "Raise your words, not voice. It is rain that grows flowers, not thunder."

AVOID MAKING GROUNDLESS PREDICTIONS

The third year of law school is less about studying and more about finding a post-graduation job. Neither of my summer internships led to any job offers. As a solid middle-of-the-pack student, my school's career center was unhelpful. Higher education "Career Centers" should be renamed "Top 10% Placement Centers." I had to pave my own way with the other 90%.

During my last semester at Brooklyn, a classmate got his hands on a list of New Jersey Superior Court judges in Passaic County who were accepting resumes for one-year clerkships. These jobs were often reserved for daughters, sons and friends of lawyers who knew a judge or knew-someone-who-knew-a-judge. I sent resumes to all of them, but only heard back from one for an interview. He was the Honorable Judge Frank M. Donato, who explained my resume leaped out at him because he and his wife had just returned from a trip to Hungary and they really liked the country. He was also intrigued by my musical background. We hit it off and he offered me the job at the end of the interview.

I moved from Manhattan back to Teaneck and began my judicial clerkship in September 1998. The job was relatively low-paying as far as legal work goes, but the hours were good (out by 4:30 pm) and Judge Donato took the end-time seriously since he religiously played golf after work.

Judicial clerks' primary task was dealing with hundreds of weekly motions, but we also performed research, sat in on trials, and were sounding boards for judges. I shared a cramped office with Mike DeMarco, who clerked for another judge. His dad was a popular lawyer and Mike knew everyone. He was unusually entertaining and emblematic of the fast-talking and witty Italians around the courthouse, later made popular by the locally-filmed Sopranos that debuted in January 1999, a few months into our clerkship term.

Maria, the Judge's secretary, was a drop-dead gorgeous Italian woman. Lawyers came up with absurd excuses to visit the Judge's office – otherwise known as his "chambers" –just to hang out with Maria. She'd be routinely gifted with flowers and chocolates, back when you could do that type of thing without needing to fill out all kinds of government-required requisitions and forms. Our chambers was a popular beehive of activity thanks to Maria.

Inside the courtroom, Judge Donato presided over only civil cases and the caseload was intriguing and steady. In one groundwater contamination case we had big-firm lawyers from all around the country descend upon the courthouse arguing about insurance coverage issues, reminiscent of scenes from a John Grisham novel. This was quite a contrast to another matter where a self-represented individual urged Judge Donato to "re-screw" himself (instead of recuse himself).

But perhaps the most interesting case before Judge Donato that year involved an inmate serving time for welfare fraud. He sued the county jail claiming he slipped in a puddle of water from a leaky toilet in the middle of the night, "cracking" his penis. The defense's theory was that the crack – or fracture – was probably the result of some rough jail sex instead. To my shock, the jury bought the story and awarded him $60,000.

The O.J. Simpson criminal trial and the "jailbreak" case underscore that you can never really predict what a jury is going to do. None of us observing the "case of the cracked penis" trial could have guessed that six jurors would unanimously decide to award even a dime to that inmate. I always roll my eyes when pundits or so-called "experts" try to predict with any certainty the outcome of a jury trial or an election. When we let the "people" speak, we usually have no idea what they're going to say.

As a postscript, I later read that the gentleman who was awarded $60,000 was soon thereafter implicated in the murder of a prostitute and was found guilty and is now serving a life sentence.

SHOOT STRAIGHT IN YOUR RELATIONSHIPS

I could write a whole book about my wife and our relationship.
I know this aspect of life doesn't work out well for everyone.
Some people never find the right partner – they either strike
out or it just doesn't happen. Others only find love during their
third marriage – as I recently heard a guy happily married with
his third wife say, "I married my wives in the wrong order."
That's one way of looking at it.

I first met my wife, Beatrix (Trixie) Nagy, in 1989 when my
Életfa band played in Toronto. Two years my junior, she was
14 years old at the time and a dancer with Toronto's Kodály
Ensemble. We'd see each other at events over the years, but it
was friendly and platonic.

When I played a gig in 1998 in Montreal, Trixie was studying
social work at McGill University and caught my eye. I finally
realized how absolutely gorgeous, smart and zestful she was.
I am still embarrassed I didn't see it before. We began
long-distance dating, visiting each other every two weeks.

We got engaged in the summer of 1999. The engagement was
magnificent. I wrote her an original song and recorded all the
instruments and voices in a professional studio. I played the
tape for her on a classic "Walkman" with headphones while we
sat on a bench near her childhood home. Towards the end of
the song, the lyrics (in Hungarian) said, "Be my wife," which
is the moment I slipped the engagement ring on her. The ring
had originally belonged to my grandmother Sarolta who had

given it to my mother. I haven't yet heard any guy one-up the romance of that moment!

Trixie moved with me to Teaneck. We rented a house my parents had purchased as an investment a few years before. Trixie started attending the M.B.A. (Marketing) program at Seton Hall University. Though it was well over 20 years ago, I still remember the giddy feeling of being fortunate enough to sleep in the same bed as Trixie every night after our extended 18-month long-distance relationship. I never take the privilege for granted, even now.

Trixie comes from classic Hungarian stock. Her dad, Zoltán (George) Nagy, has Transylvanian roots dating back centuries. He emigrated to Canada after World War II, studied chemical engineering at the University of British Columbia and worked for DuPont and the Ontario government. Trixie's mom, Beatrix, had limited career opportunities in Hungary because her biological father had been an army officer in the anti-communist Horthy regime and her adoptive father took part in the 1956 Revolution and had been jailed by the communists. In the mid-1960's, George was searching for a wife from the old country and began a penpal relationship with Beatrix, a distant relative through marriage.

In 1968, Beatrix left Hungary for Canada, emigrated to Toronto, married George and worked as a fashion buyer and a language teacher. George ruled over his family with an iron fist and their relationship did not fare well. Beatrix divorced him in the early 1980's. Sadly, she passed away in 2020.

Trixie and I got married in New Brunswick, New Jersey in April 2001. The maid of honor was Trixie's older sister, Chrysta, then pregnant with her daughter Juliet. Chrysta's son, Noah, was the ring-bearer. The Church ceremony was followed by a spectacular party with nearly 300 guests, featuring a six-piece band of Roma musicians from the Transylvanian village of Szászcsávás. Equinox, my rock musician buddies from law school, played as well. So did the members of Életfa and the Tamburitzans. The start of our new life together was marked by a music festival for the ages.

I don't profess to be a relationship expert, but if you want a tip, always be truthful with your partner and expect nothing less from your counterpart. In his wildly popular book, *The 7 Habits of Highly Effective People*, Steven Covey correctly warns, "unclear expectations will lead to misunderstanding, disappointment, and withdrawals of trust." Be clear, shoot straight.

MAKE OTHERS LOOK GOOD

Straight shooters enjoy making others look good. They don't feel the need to always take credit or minimize others.

My first job as a lawyer was as an associate for Melli, Guerin & Melli, an insurance defense firm in Paramus, New Jersey. Firms like Melli often draw new associates from judicial clerks whose one-year terms are expiring. I had sent out many resumes looking for jobs while I was a clerk for Judge Donato. One of Melli's partners who had frequently appeared in front of

Judge Donato hired me. My legal career officially kicked off in September 1999.

Melli's lawyers were appointed by insurance companies to represent drivers sued for allegedly causing accidents. Insurance defense jobs don't pay too well compared with traditional "white shoe" or "big law" firms, but they provide associates with real litigation and trial experience early on. It's a high turnover practice because of the pay and somewhat repetitive nature of the case load.

It's widely said that you can't put a value on human life, but that's exactly what insurance defense work is all about. My job was to spoon feed our claim adjusters relevant information about the plaintiff – age, education, income, nature of injury, dependents. They would put a dollar price range on that specific plaintiff's case and it was our job to try to resolve the case at the bottom end of that range. In this context, there absolutely is a value on human life. It's a whole practice area – called personal injury law.

You've seen commercials and billboards featuring celebrity lawyers on the plaintiff's side. Well, they are fighting against much lower-profile attorneys from firms like Melli. The firm's lawyers would meet every afternoon at 5:00 pm and we would be assigned motions, court conferences and depositions to attend the following day. The reason we'd only meet at 5:00 pm was because hearings would always be moved, adjourned, cancelled, or added during the day, so the next day's calendar only became clear after the close of business hours. With this approach, we weren't given much time to prepare. This was trial-by-fire on a daily basis. The best way to learn.

For one of my first assigned conferences, I was sent to a mandatory pre-trial mediation conference overseen by Judge Patrick Fitzpatrick in Bergen County. He was wildly effective in settling the most complex of cases. It's reported he settled about 30,000 cases in his 13 years on the bench. Judge Fitzpatrick understood the perspectives of the litigants and lawyers without knowing any details of the case or personalities involved. He had a wicked combination of experience and emotional intelligence.

At my first conference, Judge Fitzpatrick suggested I call my adjuster client on the payphone in the hallway and tell him the Judge was insisting on a settlement number that we all knew the client would refuse to pay. But he also told me to wait in the hallway for 10 minutes after I hung up with the client and call back again with the good news that I managed to talk the judge down to a lower number. That case settled right away.

Judge Fitzpatrick would not only ease clients into uncomfortable settlements, but also make fresh-faced associates in their first few weeks of practice look like heroes. That's how you clear over 2,000 cases a year from your docket.

If you're confident in your own skills and comfortable in your own skin, you should have no problem trying to make others look good whenever you can. It's one of the great hallmarks of a trustworthy straight shooter who exhibits great leadership and positive people management.

WATCH WHAT YOU DRIVE

Back when I worked as in-house lawyer, a group of higher-ups went out to lunch. Returning to the office they noticed a flashy red Lamborghini parked outside the front door. One of them asked the receptionist, "Whose car is that?" She responded that it belonged to one of the vendors supplying the company with mugs, t-shirts, or something-or-other.

Riding up the elevator, the management team made an immediate decision to terminate the relationship with the Lamborghini owner and find another vendor. If he could afford a flashy red Lamborghini, then the markups were clearly too high and the company was overpaying for whatever he was selling.

Years later one of my clients on the verge of bankruptcy pulled into my law firm's parking lot in a new Lexus. He asked me whether the car he parked next to – an aging two-door Toyota Yaris – was mine. He figured it was, based on the "H" (Hungary) sticker on the back. I replied that it was. He responded, "I respect your humble choice of vehicle, not often you see that from a lawyer."

I'm not sure if that was intended as a compliment, but I had to restrain myself from reminding him that his choice of vehicle might have a correlation to his insolvent status. Instead, I used it as a marketing opportunity, telling him that my favorable hourly rate compared to others with my experience might be reflected in what I was driving.

My choice in vehicle is not accidental. When contemplating leaving my in-house job and starting my own firm, I asked a legal recruiter friend to explain why lawyers who make the leap to solo practice often fail, only to find themselves back at another large firm or company. He said that many lawyers making the move still think they need all the trappings of a big firm. They lease the corner office on the 58th floor; they hire a secretary, paralegal and associate without any work to give them; and they don't watch their expenses, including their car lease rates.

In general, the main difference between an experienced lawyer charging $325/hour and an equally experienced lawyer who charges $850/hour might be boiled down to this: The more expensive lawyer has fancier furniture, nicer artwork in the office and a more expensive car in the parking lot. It doesn't mean that either billable hour rate is right or wrong, but it does explain why lawyers who work in large, lofty law firms who bill at $850/hour might suddenly begin charging $325/hour when they move to a smaller firm. And they might be even more profitable!

Once I had a meeting at the famous corporate headquarters of Walmart in Bentonville, Arkansas. I was there to discuss some litigation matters for a client together with Walmart's in-house counsel. Flying into the small city, I was struck by what a middle-of-nowhere feel Bentonville had. The building costs and taxes Walmart pays in Bentonville are fractions of what other conglomerates pay in Silicon Valley, New York or Los Angeles.

Walmart's headquarters' buildings and their layout are extremely no-frills, stressing an open concept and cubicles as opposed to closed offices. Every aspect of the campus seemed to underscore Walmart's "Save Money" slogan. When your local Walmart sells something for $1.97 rather than $1.99, keep in mind that the initial source of the $0.02 you save is the design of its Bentonville headquarters.

If you're buying, question all markups. If you're supplying, be humble about your margins. Straight shooters know that flaunting your piece of the pie is a bad idea. One great Texas lawyer I know put it this way: "Pigs get fat, but hogs get slaughtered."

SHOOT STRAIGHT EVEN WHEN THE ODDS ARE AGAINST YOU

"What are my chances of success?" This is a question that clients embroiled in litigation love to ask. But lawyers are notoriously reluctant to answer it.

The traditional cop-out answer is a variation of "50-50," "better than 50%," or "less than 50%." Each is relatively unhelpful for clients who are simply trying to determine whether spending further legal fees might be worthwhile in comparison to their chances of prevailing. At the same time, it's often practically impossible to provide a straight answer to such a question.

A strategically thinking lawyer I used to work with would answer the question quite creatively. He would give very particular numbers. I heard him approximate a "37.5%" chance of success on a motion and "63%" chance of success at trial.

These seemed to be shockingly definite numbers. And the clients were always impressed with their precision.

When I challenged him on the source of these numbers, he explained that clients held contempt for the boilerplate "50-50" answer. He thus turned to the sizzle of unequivocal numbers which were close enough to 50% to hedge. The clients loved the 37.5% and 63% numbers and uniformly would say, "now that's a straight-shootin' lawyer."

Sometimes you can get away with being specific as opposed to correct. But even when it's tough, the best policy is to always shoot straight.

PRINCIPLE #8
ALWAYS BE SCANNING

"The most pathetic person in the world is someone who has sight but no vision." - Helen Keller

Opportunities only arise if we are actively scouring for them. This makes complete sense theoretically, but actually putting it into practice has drastically multiplied the zest in my life.

Several years ago, I attended the multi-day Landmark Forum, an extremely useful self-development course. Landmark is routinely offered around the world in most major cities. It's been maligned a bit as a cult but having been through it personally, I can tell you that it's not. In fact, it revolutionized my life.

The primary bedrock of Landmark is learning to scan for "blind spots." These are things in life you don't know that you don't know, as opposed to things you know you know (like the time) or things you know you don't know (like quantum physics). We're oblivious to these blind spots because we don't know that we don't know them. Yet they end up limiting us because they stand in our way and block our progress in life.

Blind spots are typically from your past. During the Landmark course, witnessing people coming to terms with them is the seminar's emotional centerpiece. It is the key "breakthrough" the course is designed to deliver. The more dramatic blind spots uncovered are traumatic events or unhealthy relationships that have been tucked far away into attendees' memories and then are magically revealed through the help of prodigious coaching.

Luckily, I never experienced this type of trauma in my relatively serene upbringing. The blind spot I unlocked was a bit more subtle.

I learned that in my never-ending quest to keep people entertained and fill voids of silence, I was bypassing opportunities to ask others truly meaningful questions and to listen quietly and effectively. This was limiting my ability to engage in powerful, life-altering exchanges.

Through my work in Landmark, I embraced the prospect of asking non-leading questions during conversations and then shutting up, opening my mind and listening intently without any preconceived notion or preformed judgment. My breakthrough was about learning how to have potentially uncomfortable and therefore radically illuminating conversations that could expand my field of vision.

It sounds simple. Everyone knows we learn more by listening than by speaking. But that has never come easy to me and I'm still a work in progress. Something is only a "breakthrough" if there's also follow-through. So far the results have been spectacular. Dramatic improvements have occurred in my personal relationships with my wife, children, family and friends, as well as in my business and career development.

Scanning for potential blind spots is useful in many facets of life. As drivers and pedestrians, we ought to always be aggressively scanning with our eyes and ears to stay safe. In the business world, we should aim to always be scanning the landscape for potential collaborations with others as well as to effectively compete.

In his international bestseller *What They Don't Teach You at Harvard Business School*, Mark McCormack wrote: "Companies with the greatest market share often have a tendency to 'sit on a lead'. They will take solace in their numbers, become complacent, and lose their competitive edge." How right he is. See, for example, Blockbuster and Polaroid.

Helen Keller was an author and educator who became blind and deaf from an illness in her second year of life. She called "pathetic" those who had the gift of seeing but still didn't have vision. As someone who was blind, Ms. Keller still had vision. She understood that vision comes from scanning, and not merely from seeing. Always be scanning for blind spots. There's more to a zestful life than the naked eye can ever see.

DO YOU WANT YOUR BOSS' JOB IN TEN YEARS?

I've left three jobs in my life. My departures were the result of asking: "Do I want my boss's job in ten years?"

The question is not meant to be critical of who my bosses were or what they did. It's about asking whether what they were doing was right for me when projecting a decade ahead. I would expect those working for me at my own law firm to ask themselves the same question, too. It's not personal.

Though content at Melli, Guerin & Melli, I knew that litigating rear-end accidents and uninsured motorist claims was not something I was interested in doing in ten years. I started putting out feelers and sending resumes after a year at my insurance defense firm. It was the first job I ever quit and knew it was an important decision.

I was called for an interview by a litigation group at Bressler, Amery & Ross, a firm with about 100 lawyers headquartered in Florham Park, New Jersey with a small Manhattan office at the time. My resume initially caught the eye of a gentle, soft-spoken female partner who was passionate about linguistics and music – a fortuitous connection that got me in the door. Unique skills and rare interests on a resume won't connect with every prospective employer, but when they do resonate with a potential boss, the connection is usually profound. The firm hired me as an associate in 2001.

My litigation group mainly represented automotive dealers nationwide in disputes with manufacturers. We went up against the likes of Ford, Honda and BMW, represented by some of the country's top law firms. The team wasn't run by the soft-spoken partner I initially connected with but by a no-nonsense military veteran with combat experience. He governed with exacting military precision.

Excellence was demanded; every document needed to be free of typos, with no wasted words; extraordinary client responsiveness was required; and we fought hard on every procedural point. Opinions were not withheld on someone's work. This was "legal boot camp," with associates broken down and built back up. It was a management style not meant for everyone. A few associates opted out from the group rather quickly. It wasn't necessarily my ideal situation either. But the expectation for top-notch work and client responsiveness are now part of my core values thanks to that training I received relatively early in my career.

My wife and I moved to Morris County, first to the hills of Rockaway and then to vibrant Morristown where our first two kids were born. When considering whether I wanted the job of a big firm partner ten years down the line, the answer was a resounding "no." There were too many partners to contend with and an over-emphasis on billable hours versus value to the client. However, the pay at Bressler was good, I found my stride at the firm, enjoyed a short commute, worked out of a nice office with a view of the woods, provided for mouths to feed at home, and had a mortgage to pay. On balance, it was a very good job.

Six years at Bressler, Amery & Ross flew by. During the last few years, I had a feeling a big shift was imminent.

SPECIALIZE IN THE UNIQUE

As you scan for opportunities to stand out and excel in a certain area, would you rather be a small fish in a big sea, or a big fish in a small sea? There's no right answer. But I've observed that being a "big fish in a small sea" seems to provide the most potential for opportunities and growth, even though that might be counterintuitive.

At Manhattan School of Music, I was lost in a sea of excellent violinists. When I switched to viola at the age of 14, I quickly rose to become the principal violist in the school's most senior orchestra. I started to get asked to play in other orchestras. I was even called in to pinch-hit on the viola for a city-wide youth orchestra that played a concert at Lincoln Center's Alice Tully Hall, featuring the legendary French cellist Paul Tortelier playing one of the alluring Saint-Saëns cello concertos. It was among my orchestral career highlights.

Viola is a less often played instrument and in greater demand in the classical music world. Violists swim in a small sea. Ask a violinist, how do you get to Carnegie Hall? Practice, or switch to viola.

This approach also played out in the life of my daughter, Csenge, who was born in September 2003. She grew up studying the violin, but once she switched to viola in her early teens, a whole new world of opportunities opened up for her. She gained acceptances to the Bartok Conservatory of Music in Budapest where she studied for a year during high school and then to the prestigious Toronto Symphony Youth Orchestra. She is a marvelous musician and I love listening to her play. Her musical advancement has certainly been propelled forward as a result of her instrument switch.

Specializing in something unique might be risky, but it could also get you some notoriety if it pays off. The most notable stage review I ever received came from the *New York Times* in 1994, for a show I played with the Tamburitzans: "Much of the music was played on traditional and homemade instruments.

One, a curious looking trumpet-violin, was inspired by the introduction of the gramophone to Transylvania. The strangely Celtic-sounding music was performed by Kalman Magyar Jr., who stood out for his warmth and musical versatility."

The *Pittsburgh Post-Gazette's* review of the same production echoed the sentiment: "The versatile Kalman Magyar Jr. displayed his mastery of many ethnic instruments rarely heard in concert, including the intriguing Transylvanian trumpet-violin and the eerily beautiful fujara of Slovakia."

I've always been open to learning different instruments – my palette has stretched from the piano, bass guitar and drums to the seldom-heard hurdy-gurdy, Transylvanian 3-string "kontra" and the "percussive cello" of the Carpathian Mountains. The trumpet-violin and fujara are just two of the odd instruments I was asked to learn and play in the Tamburitzans. The players of such instruments in the U.S. swim in a pond, not even a sea. Yet it's enough of a pond to get good reviews in the national press. And keep in mind that it's harder to drown in a pond as opposed to in a sea.

Marketing experts have recently started writing more about how creating products and services in a niche area might actually be a better long-term strategy than marketing to the masses. Lawyers specializing in very specific practice areas or industries might have a smaller potential client base, but they tend to be the go-to counsel to that base.

If you're experiencing stagnation, maybe it's time to swim in a smaller body of water. Keep scanning for possibilities to specialize and you just might get noticed.

QUESTION WHAT YOU READ

Scanning means paying attention to the world around you, including keeping up with the news and current events. Getting straight news is a challenge. I usually have a difficult time believing anything I read or see in the news, with good reason. Having had first-hand involvement in several events and legal cases reported on by the media, I've found that none of the stories about them was ever completely accurate. It's troubling that if reporters can't get the facts right, how can we ever be expected to rely on them?

This, of course, is an issue that has been highlighted in the last few years as many media organizations seem to have become increasingly politically slanted as well. In addition to factual inaccuracy, now we also see complications with the skewed way those facts are presented (or not presented), which could be even more troubling.

An even greater transgression than inaccurate or politically slanted reporting might be when otherwise well-meaning journalists adopt language which is empty rhetoric or, even worse, just plain lazy or silly. I hope you'll pardon me for this slight tangent but just google the term "president's handpicked attorney general." You will see scores of news reports from supposedly first-rate publications criticizing the fact that U.S. Presidents have "handpicked" their AGs. The implication is that, somehow, a U.S. President should not be "handpicking" an AG. This is ludicrous. Article II of the U.S. Constitution directs that Presidents must "nominate, and by and with the Advice and Consent of the Senate, shall appoint...Officers of the United States." This is clarified to apply to AGs specifically in Title 28 of the U.S. Code, Section 503: "The President shall appoint, by and with the advice and consent of the Senate, an Attorney General of the United States. The Attorney General is the head of the Department of Justice."

By definition, every AG must be handpicked by the President. If the AG is not handpicked by the President, then she's no AG at all. Disparaging the fact that an AG is "handpicked" by the President is as absurd as referring to the President's "handpicked" Supreme Court Justice or a Mayor's "handpicked" Police Chief. These positions don't exist without the chief executive's handpicking. Nor does a corporate CEO's position exist without it being "handpicked by the Board," another doozy I've seen repeatedly. "Handpicked" is one of those trigger terms that should usually be given scrutiny.

How about the oft-repeated mantra delivered ad nauseam during the COVID-19 pandemic – "follow the experts." Really? Litigators all know that if there's an expert in support of one conclusion, you can find another expert in support of the opposite conclusion. They don't call most commercial litigation "a battle of the experts" for nothing.

Lawyers are by and large discerning and finnicky readers and listeners. I remember my own transformation as a reader as I went through law school. By my third year I was picking apart *Sports Illustrated* articles and restaurant menus – their logic, flow, evidential underpinning, and typos. Discovering that I was developing this skill was one of the real revelations of undergoing legal training.

Read as much as you can but read critically. Always question what you read and call "bull" when you see it. Yes, even – and maybe especially – what's in this very book.

LOOK FOR SPACES. ALL DAY.

At the end of high school, my father received an unexpected opportunity to attend college for free. He wasn't scanning for it but luckily it just fell on his lap.

Back when my dad was a kid, Hungary boasted international soccer's "Golden Team" (Aranycsapat), with an undefeated record for six years except for its only loss, which was at the 1954 World Cup final. Unsurprisingly he had played soccer with his buddies on the street but had no formal technical training. Because soccer was in its infancy in the U.S. in the 1960's, my dad stood out as "highly skilled" compared with his American classmates when he joined George Washington High School's soccer team in Manhattan. Mostly just immigrants played soccer in New York those days, so even a hobbyist player from a powerhouse like Hungary was an oddity in America, like a baseball player in Budapest.

As one of the more advanced high school soccer players in the city, he was recruited by a few colleges. Long Island University gave him a NCAA Division I soccer scholarship. He wasn't a standout by any means but held his own. His team made it to the NCAA Final Four twice, losing to the University of San Francisco in the 1966 finals. My dad was even inducted into the Long Island University sports hall of fame.

My favorite soccer team growing up was the New York Cosmos who played in Giants Stadium. My dad took me to several games in the early 1980's before the team was dismantled. Legends like the Brazilian Carlos Alberto, the German Franz Beckenbauer, and the Italian Giorgio Chinaglia adorned the Cosmos lineup during those days. I began observing how soccer players constantly swivel their heads, "scanning" the pitch to see where they fit in the field of play to exploit opportunities in otherwise limited space. The legends I saw early-on were experts at scanning. It's not something you can easily detect watching games on TV, but live at a stadium it becomes obvious.

My son, Soma, was born in October 2006 and has been playing soccer since he was three. It was through his experience I came to learn about the "relative age effect" in sports, which gives the competitive edge to players born earlier in the calendar year, since they're grouped by year of birth. He often competes against kids who are almost a year older than him. That's a competitive disadvantage for Soma, but a good tool for his development. He is already a better soccer player than my father or me.

I became pretty involved in Soma's soccer progression, first as a team manager and then volunteer coach. I also joined the board of directors of Toronto High Park Football Club, Soma's boyhood club, becoming Vice President of Football, providing invaluable insight into the technical part of the game and the planning that goes into it. It's through some of this technical work where I heard about sports science researchers actually analyzing scanning, called "visual exploratory behaviors." Xavi, one of the greatest midfielders of all time, was found to average 8.3 scans during the 10 seconds before he received a pass. As he explained it to *The Guardian* in 2011: "Think quickly, look for spaces. That's what I do: look for spaces. All day. I'm always looking. All day, all day."

If it works on the football pitch, it must work off it, too. Always be scanning, all day.

LONG-TERM SCANNING

Moving to Toronto was always a part of the longer-term plan with my wife since we got married. But I was only admitted to practice law in New York and New Jersey. Legal qualifications don't travel well across borders. Had I taken and passed the Ontario bar exam before moving, I would be qualified for no more than a first-year job in the Toronto market.

No Canadian firm or corporation wanted to even interview me. Yet I was still attracted to the idea of living in Toronto, consistently ranked as one of the world's most multicultural and livable cities. I wanted my wife to enjoy more time with her family and friends. The question was how to make it happen.

After several years of scanning through possibilities, not getting call-backs, and nearly giving up on the move altogether, I made contact with a legal recruiter about a potential job with Toronto's Iovate Health Sciences. Iovate is one of those sleeper companies you've never heard of. It develops and markets the world's most popular nutritional and weight management supplements, including Hydroxycut and MuscleTech branded products. Iovate was looking for an in-house lawyer to add to its legal team, mainly to manage litigation and regulatory issues in the U.S. Amazingly, admission to the Ontario bar was not a requirement. They wanted a real U.S. lawyer. It was probably one of the only U.S.-specific legal jobs in Canada, ever.

Gavin Bogle, the company's General Counsel, had previously worked in the U.S. His wife was also Hungarian and they had recently moved to Toronto to be closer to her family. We had a slew in common and we clicked. After my initial meeting with all the executives and a few trips to Toronto, I got the offer. The salary for my Assistant General Counsel role was actually a bit less than I was making as an associate, but I finally had a job in Toronto. Our move in 2007 with my wife and two small kids was a shock for my law firm colleagues at Bressler, Amery & Ross, my family, and the local Hungarian community. But the decision was ultimately pivotal for my career.

Working at Iovate was fascinating. I got to know the business intimately and became a specialist in dietary supplement law. Never did I think that I'd be dealing directly with the U.S. Food and Drug Administration and Federal Trade Commission while managing such a diverse portfolio of high-stakes cases, from class actions in San Diego to patent infringement matters in Boston. Really delving into every aspect of one single client's dealings is one of the gifts of in-house practice. The other is not filling out timesheets.

Scanning takes patience and a long-term view of its benefits is required. Xavi could swivel his head once every second and even then he wouldn't always receive a pass. But when he finally did, the pitch was under his control. I nearly gave up on scanning for possibilities in the Toronto legal market when the Iovate job popped up out of nowhere and transformed my life. If you feel your scanning is not paying off, just hang in there. Opportunities will come. Just keep scanning. Every day.

PRINCIPLE #9
MAINTAIN READY POSITION

"In the fields of observation, chance favors only the prepared mind." - Louis Pasteur

The previous chapter was all about scanning to identify opportunities. This one is about maintaining ready position so you can pounce on those opportunities. Zestful living requires a commitment to maintaining ready position so you are prepared to act when called on.

I've loved playing tennis since I was a kid. The first lesson I had was much later, on my honeymoon in St. Lucia. My wife and I have since become quite serious about it, competing in doubles leagues and playing as often as we can. Several years ago we attended a three-day tennis camp for adults at the famous IMG Academy in Bradenton, Florida. My cousin, Andrea, and her husband in nearby Sarasota watched over our kids as we were put through a backbreaking routine of warm-ups, drills and games. This was the first time in my life I was glad not to have experienced the life of a professional athlete.

Our coaches emphasize the importance of taking a "split-step" immediately before an opponent hits the ball. This is the "get ready for anything" move – setting our balance so we can react to our adversary's shot. We can then slide to the left, leap to the right, run back, sprint forward. With the racquet properly positioned at an upward angle as we split-step, we're in textbook "ready position."

Most every sport has this type of move. "Stay on your toes" is the often-repeated refrain in youth sports. It's good advice.

Life, in general, requires us to be in "ready position" and on our toes, prepared for anything. We never know when and how our next opportunity, chance, adventure will arise. Being in a position ready for motion is crucial.

Consider whether you're in a ready position – mentally, physically, emotionally. Are you actively staying on your toes, or are you apathetically drifting through life? In *Secrets of the Millionaire Mind*, Canadian-born T. Harv Eker reminds us: "It's not enough to be in the right place at the right time. You have to be the right person in the right place at the right time."

None of the other principles in this book will lead to any results unless you maintain ready position.

PUT YOURSELF IN A POSITION TO HELP OTHERS

A few years ago, I played at a Hungarian folkdance event in Washington, D.C. At one of the breaks, a very nice older guy approached me and we started talking. He was clearly an immigrant and looked very Hungarian – moustache, round face, good posture. He had a Hungarian accent yet chose to speak English because he no longer spoke Hungarian fluently. It's one of those funny situations with certain Hungarian immigrants who have largely forgotten Hungarian but haven't yet learned English fully. They're stuck in an odd linguistic limbo.

He explained that he used to be a professional dancer in Budapest and was a member of the world-famous Hungarian State Folk Ensemble in the 1960's. They toured the U.S. in the mid-60's with their last stop in New York City where they performed several shows.

During these final performances he met a young up-and-coming folk dance group director from New York who had managed to get backstage at every show. This gregarious fellow watched each show from the wings of the stage, sometimes even taking notes on the choreographies. He was an outgoing guy who would hang out at the group's hotel after the shows. The two dancers got to know each other over a few days.

That young up-and-coming dancer from New York was my father.

As it turned out, my father's newly found acquaintance wanted to defect to the U.S. This was something of a fad with dancers touring with groups from communist countries, the most high-profile being Mikhail Baryshnikov's defection to Canada while on tour with the Bolshoi Ballet in 1974. In a small world connection, my wife's ballet teacher in Toronto, Bella Kovarsky, taught Baryshnikov at the famed Vaganova Ballet Academy in St. Petersburg several years before her star pupil defected.

The 1960's marked the height of communism and Hungarian government-paid "chaperones" traveled with the large group to make sure no one tried to pull a Baryshnikov. If you were caught you'd be certainly jailed when you got back home. And if you had a U.S.-based accomplice with family members in Hungary like my dad, they'd likely be paid unfortunate visits from governmental types too.

After the group's last show, my father's friend set up an elaborate plan. He asked my father to come up to the hotel room, take his suitcase down the elevator and out of the hotel and down the block, and he'd meet my father after slithering out of the hotel empty-handed so the hypervigilant "chaperones" wouldn't notice the escape. Despite the risks, my father agreed to help his new acquaintance. The plan worked.

The man escaped from suppressive communist Hungary to freedom in America.

The two kept in touch for a brief few years after the episode but went their separate ways. Eventually the man became a prominent professor of ballet at an east coast university. It wasn't too far a drive from my gig in Washington, D.C. Our conversation got teary-eyed as he expressed gratitude for my father's help.

Perhaps the best part of the story is that I didn't hear it from my father, but from the man whose life he had changed. When I asked my dad why he never shared this story with me, he responded that it never came up in our conversations and he basically forgot about it.

Maintaining ready position will enable you to help yourself but also others. Of course, you're not supposed to be a punching bag for favors and requests from friends and family. But you generally know how to recognize those moments and situations when people need real help. That's when we're called to jump in and do what we can to assist.

When people are in need of help, provide that help. Do it selflessly. And if you do it right, you might even forget about it.

BE ON TIME

If you can't be on time, you can't maintain ready position. Being on time displays respect for others and yourself. It puts us in a mindset ready for action. It's one of the few things in life we can control – absent some truly unforeseeable event.

Being on time doesn't mean being early. Try not to arrive at 9:35 for a 10:00 meeting. I believe the proper time to arrive for an appointment is about 5 minutes early, because arriving too on-the-nose might make people uneasy. Once I played double bass for a Romanian ensemble accompanying the Mark Morris Dance Group at the Brooklyn Academy of Music and a dress rehearsal was scheduled for 5:00. I hit massive New York City traffic on the way to the theater but managed to arrive into the orchestra pit, with the bass in-hand ready to play precisely at 5:00. Mr. Morris called me out in front of the whole dance company, saying I was late. No use arguing with one of the world's most famous choreographers. I was too on-the-nose that time.

Have you ever heard of the musical, "Phantom of the Opera"? Sure you have. Most everyone has heard of Andrew Lloyd Webber's incredible musical, one of the longest running shows in Broadway history. But I'm thinking of a different version. It was written by my former Teaneck neighbor and friend Larry

Rosen, a brilliant Juilliard-trained composer and pianist. Larry's 1990 version of the musical was in development when Lloyd Webber's version premiered on Broadway in 1988. Larry was just a little late and Lloyd Webber beat him to Phantom glory. Timing is sometimes everything.

My daughter, Bibor, was born in November 2008 in Toronto. She was due on November 14, which raised a fair bit of complexity because I was contracted to play a show for a Hungarian group in Cleveland on November 15. The organizers had extended the invitation about two years before and my presence was crucial. There was no backup plan to replace me, and there was a real possibility that I might miss the birth of our third baby if she didn't arrive on time. Bibor pulled through, or "pushed out" more exactly. My angel arrived in the world in the late afternoon on November 14. I was able to drive to Cleveland early the next morning, play the gig with my band, and drive back overnight to help check my wife and third child out of the hospital.

True to her initial arrival in our lives, Bibor takes being on time very seriously. She is a very talented dancer specializing in tap, which requires exact timing and precise footwork. She is my favorite dancer in the world and certainly has the best timing, starting from her birth. When it comes to being on time, "be like Bibor"!

TAKE EVERY OPPORTUNITY SERIOUSLY

I often advise my musician friends that you never know who is in your audience, no matter the venue or the size of the crowd.

For a few years I volunteered as the keyboardist for a Church in Toronto. A parishioner paid me a compliment one time, remarking how he "dug my chops." As it turned out, he was actually a member of Blue Rodeo, an iconic Canadian country rock band. He attended Sunday masses with his family when he wasn't touring. I had no idea there was such a musical luminary listening as I was tickling the ivories during Holy Communion. Similarly, I once played at a fundraiser in New York's Natural History Museum. Only later did I learn that Paul Simon was in the crowd.

One of my lawyer friends with whom I had clerked specializes in criminal law. New prospective clients walk up to him all the time in courtrooms after he's done with his arguments. These folks are there for their initial appearances and haven't hired a lawyer yet. While they are waiting in the gallery to have their case called, they see how adeptly skillful my friend is. They're impressed by my friend's demeanor and confidence and often retain him on the spot.

Maintaining ready position means taking every opportunity seriously with the possibility that someone like Paul Simon or your next big customer is watching or listening.

LEAP INTO ACTION

After starting work as an in-house counsel at Iovate, I couldn't imagine going back to private practice. The thought of filling out timesheets, burning the midnight oil on deadlines, and chasing down accounts receivable were a thing of the distant past. But something was gnawing at me and my in-house job just didn't feel right. I didn't even know what it was, but then I happened to read a book and listen to a podcast at exactly the right time. The clouds parted and I saw the light.

The book was Tim Ferriss' *New York Times* Bestseller *The 4-Hour Workweek*. The title sounds too good to be true, and it is. I can't do the book justice in terms of a summary and strongly encourage you to read it instead. The book opened up the prospect of a life that would allow me to be a real part of my kids' journeys as they grew up, to enjoy more mobility in life, and potentially to make even more money in the process.

The podcast I heard was the Adam Carolla Show. Carolla started podcasting just a few days after his terrestrial radio program in Los Angeles was suddenly canceled. He could've worked anywhere (he had even been one of Howard Stern's sidekicks for a while), but instead decided to build his own "pirate ship." His approach underscored that a fully employable, highly experienced person's next gig didn't necessarily have to be with yet another multinational conglomerate. Rather, the real inventiveness was to create value for the professional rather than for his employer and to become impervious to ever-changing winds – providing immunity to being canceled or fired.

In 2011, I became overwhelmed with the entrepreneurial spirit and decided to launch "Magyar Law Firm." It was a risky move for someone with three kids and a sizeable Toronto mortgage. I only had one client – Iovate, which still wanted me to help manage some litigation matters. But I crunched the numbers, controlled costs, rented a small office on Toronto's Bloor Street a few blocks from home, and hung my shingle.

The key factor regarding why, over ten years later, I'm elated with striking it out on my own is realizing that my level of happiness is closely tied to my independence. Mobility, flexibility and ability to work whenever and wherever has a direct correlation to my happiness. Growth, money and other factors, while important, do not register on my personal happiness scale as much as having that freedom. I might see things differently in the future, but that's how I view it now. So long as the operational decisions for my law practice are aligned with that notion of maintaining independence, my days are pretty good.

When asked why I decided to start my own law firm, I start with the influence of Tim's writing and Adam's voice. Many of the principles and life lessons discussed in this book are the result of reading other books and listening to interviews, but Tim and Adam hit me at exactly the right time. Be in a position to leap into action if something you read or hear connects with you. That's the moment when scanning meets ready position.

CALCULATE YOUR APPETITE FOR RISKS

Putting ourselves in a position to act sometimes requires risk taking. I've never been a big risk-taker. Come to think of it, lawyers might be one of the most risk-averse subset of people in society, which is why they're drawn to perhaps the most conservative profession in history. The leading model for running a law firm is over 100 years old, a long time in terms of modern entrepreneurialism which doesn't say much about lawyers' appetite for risk. The model itself is mind-numbingly conservative. It's called the "Cravath System," named after the founding partner of a prestigious Wall Street law firm. It's premised on compensating associates on a lockstep basis based on seniority. Boring!

One of my forefathers, László Magyar, was definitely a risk taker, especially for his time. He explored remote Southwest Africa in the 19th century. László was the half-brother of Kálmán Magyar I – they had the same father, Imre Magyar, a landowner who had a propensity to impregnate women out of wedlock, including each of Kálmán I and László's mothers. László had quite the life. He was married to the daughter of the King of an Angolan province, who apparently "gifted" László a few hundred Angolan slaves to journey throughout the area with him.

My Godfather and mother's brother, Uncle Charlie (Károly), embarked on a somewhat different but still risky journey when he was only 15 years old, escaping communist Hungary with his father János through the minefields and fences of the Austrian border. He had good reason to leave Hungary. Given his family's aristocratic history, he'd been refused admission to communist-controlled public high schools. His options were limited in Hungary, with his family's past acting as an irreversible negative mark. Charlie became somewhat of an early I.T. pioneer in the financial services industry in New York. He ended up marrying my aunt Rosemary, another Hungarian immigrant who had also danced in the "Hungária" folkdance group with my parents. They had two kids but divorced. Charlie then married Barbara, whom he had met in New York's financial community when he worked at Merrill Lynch. Barbara suffered a pretty devastating stroke over ten years ago but it's heartwarming to see how Charlie cares for her. Charlie still loves to travel and experience new things and still has the adventurous spirit that led him out of Hungary so many years ago.

When it comes to my own appetite for risk, I prefer to take calculated risks, with the chance of failure built into the calculation. My biggest calculated risk was leaving in-house employment and starting my own law firm. When contemplating this move, everyone I spoke with who had profitably accomplished the transition (lawyers, accountants, drywallers, web designers, consultants) told me the following would happen, so long as I controlled costs:

- Year 1: make less money than before

- Year 2: make the same money as before

- Year 3 & onwards: make more money than before

For the most part that has panned out – for me and many others I've spoken with among a wide cluster of enterprises. Of course, there is a theoretical risk that all of my clients could gang up and decide to quit using my firm the same day. This is highly unlikely and definitely the nightmare scenario, but I've calculated that the worst that would happen is that I would need to start sending out resumes again and look for a new job with a new employer. I hope I will be in a position ready to act if that ever happens.

You've scanned. Your scanning leads to opportunity. You've maintained ready position so you're ready to act. Now, it's time to go for it. Take your shot.

Sometimes we forget that last part. Remember that if you don't take shots on net, you'll never score. Two athletes I saw play live before they retired – Wayne Gretzky and Michael Jordan – are famously quoted as saying: "You miss 100% of the shots you don't take." Yet we often continue to pass on shooting opportunities. We don't schedule that meeting. We don't cold-call that potential client. We don't apply for that job. We don't follow through on our next business idea. We don't sign up for that free online education class.

We don't take our shots because of the fear of failure. It's easier to avoid the discomfort of failure by steering clear of taking the shot altogether. But failing never stops the superstars. Michael Jordan missed 2 out of every 3 shots he took from three-point range. Wayne Gretzky's shooting percentage was less than 20%. Get comfortable with failure, it's part of the game, even for the greats. What's the worst that can happen – you'll miss your shot? Big deal! You'll just take another one.

Today, take the first step towards whatever you've been holding back from doing. If you've put yourself in a position to take that shot, take it. It's alright if you miss. If you don't fail, you're not trying hard enough. Missing shots is as much a part of zestful living as making them.

PRINCIPLE #10
CRAFT YOUR OWN FUTURE

"The future starts today, not tomorrow." - Pope John Paul II

This is the last principle and the most creative and fun one to implement. In the previous two chapters you've read about identifying opportunities and taking actions. Now you'll find out how those actions can be used to craft the future you want for yourself.

Crafting your own future is not about daydreaming. It's about putting your pants on and getting to work on something today with the long-term goal of seeing results only well into the future. This requires a patient frame of mind but it's the most secure and certain way of getting to where we want to be.

Taking the Florida bar exam and teaching business law in Naples were actions designed to put me in a position to spend increasingly more time in Florida. Currently, I'm taking small steps to later bring to fruition my goal of sitting on corporate boards in my 50's. Hopefully fortune will be kind and I'll have a bit of luck. It's pretty clear I've enjoyed my fair share of blessings as evidenced by the stories in this book. Maybe I'll be scooped up to do something I can't reasonably foresee. I'll lead a big corporation, tour the world with a famous musician, become an ambassador, or be a talk-show host.

The great Hungarian philosopher Béla Hamvas wrote in *Németség (Germanism)*: "Man is granted his life, but it is up to him to voluntarily choose how he lives it. This is how the concepts of existence, freedom, ambition, and immortality are connected." In other words, the future shouldn't be left to Roma fortune tellers and idle daydreamers. We can control more of it than we might believe.

SEEK ADVICE FROM MENTORS

Rarely embark down a specific path for the future or into a new venture without first finding a mentor in that field.

At the start of my legal career, I had a great opportunity to seek advice from an experienced lawyer – a "mentor" albeit a fleeting one. He was a well-known entertainment attorney at a powerhouse firm with offices in New York and Los Angeles. A friend introduced us because of my interest in "entertainment law" which I viewed as a perfect combination of my musical and legal backgrounds.

This wasn't a job interview. Meeting with a mentor shouldn't be one. I was full of questions about this super-lawyer's practice area, clientele, background, and how he got to be where he was.

The lawyer had just flown back on the red-eye, no doubt on business class, from Los Angeles. He rubbed his tired eyes, took a sip of coffee and said, "Let me tell you about so-called 'entertainment law.'" I was riveted.

The lawyer continued, "A contract is a contract, a lawsuit is a lawsuit. The only real difference between entertainment law and any other type of law is the name of the party at the top of the document."

It was a tremendous revelation. I needed to master contracts, litigation and other substantive aspects of the law first. The "boring" stuff. Only then could I consider building a clientele in a particular industry such as "entertainment." And ultimately the industry would never be as important as mastering the substantive legal issues in play.

Fast-forward to today, my firm has clients stretching beyond many national borders and industries. They include concert producers, theatres, publishers, artists, athletes, fashion designers, and advertisers. In other words, my practice now ranges from entertainment to international law, even though at its core it's basically mostly contracts and litigation and variations or offshoots of those two basic foundations.

Mentors can come in all forms. They don't have to be highly compensated jet setting entertainment lawyers. I learned pretty much all I know about bow technique in folk music through sporadic encounters with a virtually illiterate violinist from a Transylvanian village in the western part of Romania. These mini-lessons with the late and great Sándor "Neti" Fodor were few in quantity but decisive in quality. I engaged him in discussion whenever I saw him – at festivals, camps, concerts, or bars. He made up for a lack of formal education with unparalleled experience and an eagerness to share his philosophy of playing.

The key with mentors is to ask questions and listen with open ears. You might not hear what you expect to hear, and that's what makes a great mentor valuable to your development and planning your own future.

When we moved to Toronto in 2007, my wife and I wanted to live somewhere near the subway line and preferably on the west end of the city so it would be closer to my job. We found a newly renovated home in Bloor West Village near High Park, an historically Ukrainian area becoming overrun by lawyers, accountants and bankers. Everything was walkable within 10 minutes or less – parks, schools, churches, libraries, shopping, the subway. This type of life was highly unlikely anywhere in New Jersey. It was the Toronto my wife had told me about for years and I loved it – after getting over the sizeable price tag.

One day we received a knock on the door from HGTV, the cable network, whose producers were scouting for a show called "Four Houses Canada." During each episode, four homeowners would tour and score each other's homes and the winner came away with $1,000 cash and a small HGTV magazine picture spread. They needed a male contestant to go along with a house in the neighborhood; it sounded fun and I was in.

This was my first and only foray into reality TV. I quickly realized what a misnomer "reality TV" is. Touring a house, we'd walk into a room and have an authentic reaction to the surprises in the room. The director would yell "cut" and then ask us to react differently or in a more drastic or refined manner. The production team never quite told us what to do or what to say, but they certainly prodded us to fit their narrative.

The episode aired as the series premiere in 2012. After the points were tallied, our house had won. Six years later we decided to sell the winning home and move to a condo with underground parking and even a pool and a hot tub in the building. We love the lock-and-leave aspect to condo living, its simplicity compared to home ownership which allows us the ability to travel more flexibly.

Make yourself a home you are proud of and comfortable in. Your home might even contain your own personal "happy place," a particular location which calms you down and provides a sense of peace and quiet. Or it could be a physical location, park, couch, or coffee shop. It might not be a physical location, though – perhaps it's a mental destination arrived at through meditation or prayer. It is a place where clarity resides and ideas for the future are born.

My happy place is a specific hot tub in Naples. Here's how I got there, though the journey is not without tragedy.

Mária, one of my dad's sisters, and her husband Gyula Szalay started vacationing in Naples ages ago. Gyula was a brilliant Hungarian-educated lawyer who received straight A's through his studies. After the 1956 Revolution he and Mária emigrated to Sweden and then to the United States. Gyula became an engineer. They established Washington D.C.'s META Engineers which designed HVAC systems for large government buildings. Their family lived in a beautiful home in Rockville, Maryland, but were marred by unfathomable adversity.

In the middle of the night in 1989 our home phone rang. My dad picked it up and he did something I never saw him do before or since. He slammed on the wall with his fist in anger. It was clear the news was devastating. Gyula was on the phone explaining that his 26 year-old son, my cousin Tom Szalay, had been shot dead in a convenience store while traveling through New Orleans with his girlfriend. It shook our whole family to its core.

A few years later, Gyula and Mária endured a vicious home invasion burglary in Rockville. Three masked men broke in, tied them up together with my grandmother Sarolta, and wiped them out of valuable yet priceless jewelry and family heirlooms.

Gyula and Mária decided to move full-time to Naples. Mária died several years after their move. Gyula remarried, to another Hungarian woman ironically called Mária. But Gyula has also passed away, survived by Tom's brother, my cousin Attila.

Magda, my dad's other twin sister, met the dapper Nándor Száyer at the Camp Kilmer refugee center in New Jersey in early 1957. It was love at first sight. While Magda toiled away for decades at the Metropolitan Opera, Nándor worked as an engineer on such projects as Toronto's CN Tower and my parking pad in Rockaway, New Jersey. They also embraced the beauty of Naples after many visits to Gyula and Mária and moved there as well.

Soon after their move to Naples, Nándor passed away suddenly. Reviewing family documents after his death, we discovered a secret he kept from the family all his life. He was the Vice President of one of the student-run National Revolutionary Commissions during the 1956 Revolution in Budapest. We had no idea of his active involvement in the Revolution, but immediately understood why he would bite his lip and quietly smile when others would gloat about how many Soviets they shot at during the Revolution. Nándor was, quietly, the real deal. A true patriot who took his secret to the grave.

The ever-youthful Magda found a second love in the form of Helmut Paul, an energetic and slightly younger German immigrant to south Florida. Over the years my family stayed with them for holidays in Naples. We became huge fans of the luscious greenery, the youthfulness of the retirees we met, the opportunity to play endless amounts of tennis, and obviously the weather. My wife and I loved it so much we ended up buying a condo in Naples, with the intention of renting it out and enjoying it ourselves as our lives progress. It's our place of refuge, particularly when Toronto turns cold and grey.

There's a precise spot in the community pool's hot tub that is my "happy place." In the hot tub I sit facing the pool surrounded by a preserve with tons of palm trees. The trees alone are enough to lower my stress. Add the warm water and jets of the hot tub, and I'm all yours. I do a fair bit of clear-minded plotting for the future when I sit there.

BUILD YOUR TEAM FOR THE FUTURE

A year after I started Magyar Law Firm, my old boss at Iovate, Gavin Bogle, also left the company to start his own solo firm.

Gavin is probably the smartest person I know, with lots of experience in biotechnology, business and law. We started collaborating on several matters right away. He took on transactional and intellectual property work while I focused on litigation and dispute resolution. It was only natural that we combine our solo practices, forming Magyar & Bogle in 2014. Our ability to attract and retain clients, from both sides of the border, grew exponentially.

By a stroke of fortunate timing, I discovered that my good friend and former neighbor, Will O'Hara, was looking to leave his large law firm in downtown Toronto. Will has been practicing law for about 15 years longer than Gavin and me. He is a quintessential Canadian trial lawyer. He knows the courts and the rules of civil procedure inside-out and is a great litigation strategist. Will has even earned an accreditation of Certified Specialist in Civil Litigation by the Law Society of Ontario. He's also a skilled musician and author. It wasn't too hard to convince Will to join us as a partner.

In 2016, Magyar, Bogle & O'Hara LLP was born. Our team works together harmoniously, each of us with the confidence to offer our unique perspectives. While we might engage in vigorous debates, we are always respectful of each other.

I am well aware this is not the case at every organization. A famous example can be drawn from Walter Isaacson's epic biography *Steve Jobs* about the Apple founder: "He made a point of being brutally honest. 'My job is to say when something sucks rather than sugarcoat it,' he said. This made him charismatic and inspiring, yet also, to use the technical term, an ass-hole at times." Even though I have nothing but admiration for the way the late Steve Jobs changed the world, that dog doesn't hunt at our firm. We have a no ass-holes policy. We treat our team members with respect, just like we'd like to be treated. We emphasize giving our team members as much independence in terms of where they work and when they work, knowing it's a big factor in overall job satisfaction and efficiency. Since we all often work from other locations, we were way ahead of the remote-work trend caused by the COVID-19 pandemic and we carried on without missing a beat.

It is said that in a properly run corporation like Apple, the directors should be thinking ten years ahead; executives and officers should be thinking five years ahead; managers should be thinking one year ahead; and the remaining employees should be thinking one day ahead. It's a bit different in law firms, particularly boutique firms like ours where we wear many hats. As Managing Partner, I mainly serve as a quarterback, handing off projects to the right people, managing the workflow, and interfacing with clients in delivering what's needed.

We try to do the best possible job for current clients. We're driven by the axiom that one client is likely to refer three others, those three will refer three others to generate nine, then to 27, and up from there. This has worked in my law practice and musical ventures equally. It's a very specific action (doing good work for today's clients) that will only lead to results in the future (new referrals by today's clients).

If you prefer to be surrounded with cronies, yes-men and lapdogs – and if you think you're the only person who can get something done – Confucius has a nice warning for you: "If you are the smartest person in the room, then you are in the wrong room." I have made it a point to run my firm with colleagues that I believe are smarter and more experienced than me. There is no other professional environment I can imagine myself thriving in now or in the future.

UNDERSTAND THE PAST SO YOU CAN COMPREHEND TOMORROW

You can only know where you're going when you understand where you've been. I am certain that one of my great-grandfathers died in a Russian POW camp so his daughter could grow up tenacious enough to strongarm herself into a job at the famed Metropolitan Opera without speaking English. I am also sure that two other great-grandparents of mine had their dignity stripped away from them so their eldest son could muster the backbone to escape the grips of Communism through barbed wire fences. Without the victimization of the Hungarian people by wars and revolutions, my family would not have emigrated to the U.S. But times have evolved.

Most of my family began replanting roots in Budapest starting from the fall of the Iron Curtain in the early 1990's. My parents live in Budapest virtually full-time, blocks away from where their own lives began. Ildiko my sister also moved to Hungary several years ago with her family. Her husband, László Hajdú-Németh, worked in Morgan Stanley's New York office before his intracompany transfer to Budapest, the result of some crafty future design on his part. Their three children – László, Balázs and Ilona – have immersed themselves in Hungarian folklore and are highly proficient folk musicians and dancers. They've gained semi-stardom on the internationally televised "Fölszállott a Páva" talent show – a Hungarian folk version of "Star Search" or "So You Think You Can Dance." These kids, born in New Jersey, carry the torch of their Hungarian roots in Budapest, for the whole world to see on their screens.

It's ironic to consider the sacrifice it took for my grandparents and parents to "escape" from Hungary, only to have much of the family end up back there again. They not only understand where they've been historically, but also know where they're going – which is, in a way, right back into that history. The circle is complete.

Most of my music-making now is with the Gyanta Hungarian Folk Band based out of Ontario and Quebec. I first grasped the expanse of the U.S. through my Tamburitzans tours, but it's through journeying with Gyanta that I've experienced Canada's alluring greatness, from the French-Canadian communities of Quebec to the views of the Pacific Ocean from Victoria, and everywhere in between. Like in the old days with Életfa, we travel throughout Canada and the U.S. playing in a wide array of theatres, festivals, and Hungarian events. Our focus is the "Táncház" style of music, just like back in the 1980's.

Over the years, just to whet my musical appetite, I've engaged in other musical ventures, eclectic experiments such as Crossing Paths (ethno-jazz), Continental Dance Orchestra (Hungarian-American wedding band), and Dallam-Dougou (African-Hungarian fusion). I've entertained politicians and dignitaries at the United Nations, Embassies, Consulates, and Governors' Mansions. Over time I've been fortunate to play in many prestigious venues including B.B. King's Blues Club (NYC), Fiddler's Elbow (London, UK), Place-des-Arts (Montréal), Symphony Space (NYC), Hothouse (Chicago), Roy Thomson Hall (Toronto), Town Hall (NYC), and Heinz Hall (Pittsburgh).

But musically I'll always return to my core. Playing acoustic, microphone-free village tunes surrounded by folk dancers covered with sweat in poorly-lit Hungarian clubs will always remain at the heart of where I've been and where I'm heading.

NOW GO AND CRAFT YOUR FUTURE

The key consideration in crafting your own future is to examine what actions you can take today that will lead to where you want to be in five or ten years. Establish your plan now. But never forget the other nine principles for zestful living. Your future planning will only materialize if you abide by all ten of this book's principles.

I hope that by following these principles you will generate all of the happiness, enthusiasm, and energy you can handle – today, tomorrow, and forever. May zest be with you, always.

ACKNOWLEDGEMENTS

I am grateful to Jeremiah Brown for contributing his insightful foreword. My wife and I met him a few years ago, at a Canadian Olympic Committee reception we were invited to by a lawyer friend of mine in Toronto. There were other former Canadian Olympians there, but Jeremiah the rowing giant stood out with his biting sense of humor and outgoing presence. We bonded immediately and became friends. As a silver medallist at the 2012 Summer Olympics, he knows a thing or two (or a hundred) about putting pants on and getting to work. I am humbled by his friendship.

It's an honor that Marissa Stapley, the Toronto-based internationally bestselling author of several novels, read the final version and blessed it with her wholehearted endorsement. Having such a prominent and world-class professional reinforce the book's message gave me the comfort and confidence to put it out to the world.

My unending thanks goes out to my mentor-in-authorship from beginning to end – my law partner, musical colleague and terrific writer and author, Will O'Hara. He offered me his wisdom into effective outlining, was a consistent sounding board during the creative process, and was kind enough to review the book and suggest edits as it neared completion.

I was lucky enough to meet author and entrepreneur James Masciarelli in my "happy place" in Naples, who graciously agreed to read an early draft. His discerning and astute recommendations to the book's structure were pivotal in what later became the published version. My gratitude to James is boundless.

My parents, Judit and Kálmán Magyar, as well as my sister, Dr. Ildiko Hajdú-Németh, were instrumental in providing family-related information, photographs for the hard-copy version and ideas. They also reviewed the manuscript and provided insightful edits. I am grateful to them for their contributions to the book and my life.

Special thanks to my other advance readers who reviewed and provided insightful edits at various stages: Kathy Zimon (Fine Arts Librarian Emeritus at the University of Calgary and my wife's aunt), Elle Haneke (Toronto-based freelance writer and awesome neighbor), and James Silver (superstar lawyer, business phenom, and one of my law firm's proud alumni).

I profoundly thank my wife, Trixie (bea-trained.com), for her unending love, support and guidance during the writing process. She is a meticulous reader and wonderful writer, which makes her my perfect in-house, always-available advisor with polished judgment and perception. Just as she lights up any room, her brightness shines throughout the book as well. She will forever remain my ideal muse as we navigate our zestful lives together.

Last but never least, I thank my children – Csenge, Soma and Bibor – with intense gratitude for giving me the reason to write this book. And thanks to our dog, Pogi, for not peeing on it.